studysync®

Reading & Writing Companion

Suspense!

studysync.com

Copyright © BookheadEd Learning, LLC
All Rights Reserved.

Send all inquiries to:
BookheadEd Learning, LLC
610 Daniel Young Drive
Sonoma, CA 95476

Cover, ©iStock.com/MoreISO, ©iStock.com/GiuseppeParisi, ©iStock.com/alexey_boldin, ©iStock.com/skegbydave

9 LWI 21 20 19 C

STUDENT GUIDE

GETTING STARTED

Welcome to the StudySync Reading and Writing Companion! In this booklet, you will find a collection of readings based on the theme of the unit you are studying. As you work through the readings, you will be asked to answer questions and perform a variety of tasks designed to help you closely analyze and understand each text selection. Read on for an explanation of each section of this booklet.

Student Instructions for Reading and Writing Companion

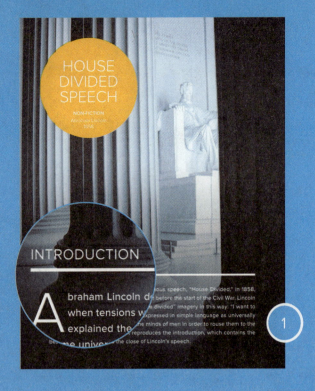

1 INTRODUCTION

An Introduction to each text provides historical context for your reading as well as information about the author. You will also learn about the genre of the excerpt and the year in which it was written.

2 FIRST READ

During your first reading of each excerpt, you should just try to get a general idea of the content and message of the reading. Don't worry if there are parts you don't understand or words that are unfamiliar to you. You'll have an opportunity later to dive deeper into the text.

Many times, while working through the Think Questions after your first read, you will be asked to **annotate** or **make annotations** about what you are reading. This means that you should use the "Notes" column to make comments or jot down any questions you may have about the text. You may also want to note any unfamiliar vocabulary words here.

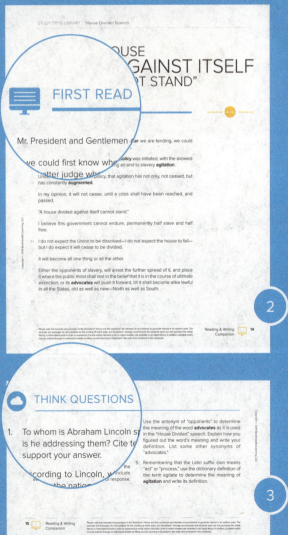

3 THINK QUESTIONS

These questions will ask you to start thinking critically about the text, asking specific questions about its purpose, and making connections to your prior knowledge and reading experiences. To answer these questions, you should go back to the text and draw upon specific evidence that you find there to support your responses. You will also begin to explore some of the more challenging vocabulary words used in the excerpt.

iv Reading & Writing Companion

Student Instructions for Reading and Writing Companion

4. CLOSE READ & FOCUS QUESTIONS

After you have completed the First Read, you will then be asked to go back and read the excerpt more closely and critically. Before you begin your Close Read, you should read through the Focus Questions to get an idea of the concepts you will want to focus on during your second reading. You should work through the Focus Questions by making annotations, highlighting important concepts, and writing notes or questions in the "Notes" column. Depending on instructions from your teacher, you may need to respond online or use a separate piece of paper to start expanding on your thoughts and ideas.

5. WRITING PROMPT

Your study of each excerpt or selection will end with a writing assignment. To complete this assignment, you should use your notes, annotations, and answers to both the Think and Focus Questions. Be sure to read the prompt carefully and address each part of it in your writing assignment.

6. EXTENDED WRITING PROJECT

After you have read and worked through all of the unit text selections, you will move on to a writing project. This project will walk you through steps to plan, draft, revise, edit, and finally publish an essay or other piece of writing about one or more of the texts you have studied in the unit. Student models and graphic organizers will provide guidance and help you organize your thoughts as you plan and write your essay. Throughout the project, you will also study and work on specific writing skills to help you develop different portions of your writing.

UNIT 1   What attracts us to stories of suspense?

Suspense!

TEXTS

4 — Let 'Em Play God
NON-FICTION *Alfred Hitchcock*

9 — The Monkey's Paw
FICTION *W.W. Jacobs*

23 — Sorry, Wrong Number
DRAMA *Lucille Fletcher*

28 — Violence in the Movies
NON-FICTION *Point/Counterpoint*

34 — A Night to Remember
NON-FICTION *Walter Lord*

40 — Cujo
FICTION *Stephen King*

46 — Lord of the Flies
FICTION *William Golding*

53 — Ten Days in a Mad-House (Chapter IV)
NON-FICTION *Nellie Bly*

Reading & Writing Companion

Please note that excerpts and passages in the StudySync® library and this workbook are intended as touchstones to generate interest in an author's work. The excerpts and passages do not substitute for the reading of entire texts, and StudySync® strongly recommends that students seek out and purchase the whole literary or informational work in order to experience it as the author intended. Links to online resellers are available in our digital library. In addition, complete works may be ordered through an authorized reseller by filling out and returning to StudySync® the order form enclosed in this workbook.

TEXTS

60	**The Tell-Tale Heart** **FICTION** *Edgar Allan Poe*
68	**Annabel Lee** **POETRY** *Edgar Allan Poe*
72	**The Bells** **POETRY** *Edgar Allan Poe*

EXTENDED WRITING PROJECT

79	Extended Writing Project: Narrative Writing
83	**SKILL:** Organize Narrative Writing
86	Extended Writing Project: Prewrite
89	**SKILL:** Introductions
91	**SKILL:** Narrative Techniques and Sequencing
96	Extended Writing Project: Plan
98	**SKILL:** Writing Dialogue
102	**SKILL:** Conclusions
105	Extended Writing Project: Draft
107	**SKILL:** Transitions
109	Extended Writing Project: Revise
111	Extended Writing Project: Edit, Proofread, and Publish

115

Text Fulfillment through StudySync

LET 'EM PLAY GOD

NON-FICTION
Alfred Hitchcock
1948

INTRODUCTION

With films that consistently put viewers on the edge of their seats, British film director Alfred Hitchcock earned the nickname "The Master of Suspense." In the following excerpt from a 1948 essay, Hitchcock describes how he creates suspense by letting the audience "play God"—by providing them with certain information not known to characters in a movie—and illustrates how he used the technique to create dramatic tension in his 1948 thriller, *Rope*.

"You have suspense when you let the audience play God."

FIRST READ

1 Every maker of mystery movies aims at getting the audience on the edge of their seats. The **ingredient** to keep them there is called "suspense." Producers cry for it, writers cry in agony to get it, and actors cry for joy when they do get it. I've often been asked what it is.

2 As far as I'm concerned, you have suspense when you let the audience play God.

3 Suppose, for instance, you have six characters involved in a mystery. A man has been murdered and all six are possible **suspects** but no one is sure including the audience.

4 One of the characters, a young man, is standing in a shadowy room with his back to the door when an unidentified character in a cloak and black hat sneaks in and slugs him into **insensibility.** It's a brutal act, but if the audience does not know whether the young man is a killer or a hero they will not know whether to cheer or weep.

5 If the audience does know, if they have been told all the secrets that the characters do not know, they'll work like the devil for you because they know what fate is facing the poor actors. That is what is known as "playing God." That is suspense.

6 For 17 years I have been making pictures described alternately as thriller, dark mysteries, and chillers, yet I have never actually directed a whodunit or a puzzler. Offhand this may sound like **debunking,** but I do not believe that puzzling the audience is the essence of suspense.

7 Take, for instance, the drama I recently filmed at Warner Bros. called *Rope*. It stars James Stewart with Joan Chandler, our new discovery, in the feminine lead.

8. John Dall and Farley Granger strangle a young man in the opening shot. They put his body in a chest, cover the chest with a damask cloth and silver service, then serve *hors d'oeuvres* and drinks from it at a party for the victim's father, mother, sweetheart, and assorted friends. Everyone is gay and charming. When Stewart begins to suspect foul play late in the film John Dall puts a gun in his pocket in case things get too hot.

9. The audience knows everything from the start, the players know nothing. There is not a single detail to puzzle the audience. It is certainly not a whodunit for the simple reason that everyone out front knows who did it. No one on the screen knows except the two murderers. The fact that the audience watches actors go blithely through an atmosphere that is loaded with evil makes for real suspense.

10. These are the questions, now, that constantly pop up. Will the murderers break and give themselves away? When the victim does not show up for the party will his father suspect? Will Jimmy get killed before he discovers the actual crime? How long will that body lie in its wooden grave at a champagne party without being discovered? If we are successful we'll have the audience at such a pitch that they want to shout every time one of the players goes near that chest.

11. In order to achieve this, one of the necessary ingredients of the formula is a series of **plausible** situations with people that are real. When characters are unbelievable you never get suspense, only surprise.

12. Just because there is a touch of murder and an air of mystery about a story it is not necessary to see transoms opening, clutching fingers, hooded creatures, and asps on the Chinese rug.

13. Spellbound was based on complete psychiatric truth. *Foreign Correspondent* was simply the story of a man hammering away at events with a woman who was not much help. *Notorious* concerned a woman caught in a web of world events from which she could not extricate herself and *The Paradine Case* was a love story embedded in the emotional quicksand of a murder trial.

14. In none of these was the house filled with shadows, the weather dull and stormy throughout, the moor windswept, and the doors creaky. In fact, it is important in a story with sinister implications to use counterpoint, great contrast between situation and background, as we did in *Rope*.

15. John Dall is guilty of a bestial crime which the audience sees him perform with young Granger. But throughout the film he is grace and charm itself and his apartment is gay and beautifully appointed. And when Granger plays the piano he picks a light and childish piece, a minuet. Suspense involves contrast.

Copyrighted 2014. Prometheus Global Media. 110650:614AT.

THINK QUESTIONS

1. From his examples, it's clear that Alfred Hitchcock expects readers to be familiar with his films. However, some readers may not have seen many or any of Hitchcock's movies. What do the examples that Hitchcock uses in paragraphs 3 and 4 tell you about the kinds of movies he made? How does paragraph 6 support your inferences? Use evidence from the text to explain your answer.

2. Based on the first five paragraphs, what is Alfred Hitchcock discussing in this essay? Hitchcock says, "I do not believe that puzzling the audience is the essence of suspense." What kinds of examples does he use to help him support that statement?

3. How does Alfred Hitchcock explain creating suspense in a film by using the example of his movie, *Rope*, starring James Stewart? Refer to one or more details from the text to support your answer.

4. Use context to determine the meaning of the word **plausible** as it is used in paragraph 11 of "Let 'Em Play God." Write your definition of "plausible" here and explain how you figured it out.

5. The Latin prefix *in-* means "not," and the word "sense" comes from the Latin root *sensus*, meaning "to feel or perceive." Use your knowledge of Latin roots and affixes, as well as context clues provided in the passage, to determine the meaning of **insensibility** in paragraph 4. Write your definition of "insensibility" and explain how you figured it out.

STUDYSYNC LIBRARY | Let 'Em Play God

CLOSE READ

Reread the excerpt from "Let 'Em Play God." As you reread, complete the Focus Questions below. Then use your answers and annotations from the questions to help you complete the Writing Prompt.

FOCUS QUESTIONS

1. In paragraph 2, the author states that in a movie, "you have suspense when you let the audience play God." Highlight text evidence and make annotations that explain how the author, film director Alfred Hitchcock, allows the audience to "play God" in his films.

2. In paragraph 5, Hitchcock says that an audience "will work like the devil" for him if he tells them all the secrets his characters do not know. What can you infer about Hitchcock's attitude toward the people who watch his movies? How does this phrase relate, or connect, to Hitchcock's purpose for writing? Highlight context clues to define the phrase, as well as text evidence that tells you how Hitchcock and his actors will know they have succeeded in engaging the audience for *Rope*.

3. How does Hitchcock feel about what he describes as "whodunit or puzzler" movies? Highlight the sentences that explain Hitchcock's point of view toward these kinds of films, and annotate to explain what Hitchcock believes is the difference between suspense and surprise.

4. In paragraph 10, Hitchcock asks a series of questions. What purpose do these questions serve in the article? What does Hitchcock mean when he says that the questions "constantly pop up"? Annotate your answer to explain your reasoning.

5. Discuss Alfred Hitchcock's article and his movie *Rope* in relation to the essential question for this unit: *What attracts us to stories of suspense?* Make annotations and highlight textual evidence that supports your ideas.

WRITING PROMPT

What does the author mean by the phrase "letting the audience play God"? Is the plot of the movie *Rope* that Hitchcock describes a good example of letting the audience "play God"? Why or why not? How does Hitchcock use the film as an illustration of his point of view? Be sure to cite textual evidence to develop your essay and support your ideas.

THE MONKEY'S PAW

FICTION
W.W. Jacobs
1902

INTRODUCTION

In "The Monkey's Paw," W.W. Jacob's cautionary tale from 1902, a well-to-do family in Victorian England is presented with a dubious opportunity to increase their fortunes. A magical monkey's paw from India has the power to make three wishes come true, but what will be the price?

"...it's just an ordinary little paw dried to a mummy."

FIRST READ

I.

1. Without, the night was cold and wet, but in the small parlour of Laburnam Villa the blinds were drawn and the fire burned brightly. Father and son were at chess, the former, who possessed ideas about the game involving radical changes, putting his king into such sharp and unnecessary perils that it even provoked comment from the white-haired old lady knitting placidly by the fire.

2. "Hark at the wind," said Mr. White, who, having seen a fatal mistake after it was too late, was amiably desirous of preventing his son from seeing it.

3. "I'm listening," said the latter, grimly surveying the board as he stretched out his hand. "Check."

4. "I should hardly think that he'd come to-night," said his father, with his hand poised over the board.

5. "Mate," replied the son.

6. "That's the worst of living so far out," bawled Mr. White, with sudden and unlooked-for violence; "of all the beastly, slushy, out-of-the-way places to live in, this is the worst. Pathway's a bog, and the road's a torrent. I don't know what people are thinking about. I suppose because only two houses in the road are let, they think it doesn't matter."

7. "Never mind, dear," said his wife, soothingly; "perhaps you'll win the next one."

8. Mr. White looked up sharply, just in time to intercept a knowing glance between mother and son. The words died away on his lips, and he hid a guilty grin in his thin grey beard.

9. "There he is," said Herbert White, as the gate banged to loudly and heavy footsteps came toward the door.

10. The old man rose with hospitable haste, and opening the door, was heard condoling with the new arrival. The new arrival also condoled with himself, so that Mrs. White said, "Tut, tut!" and coughed gently as her husband entered the room, followed by a tall, burly man, beady of eye and rubicund of visage.

11. "Sergeant-Major Morris," he said, introducing him.

12. The sergeant-major shook hands, and taking the **proffered** seat by the fire, watched contentedly while his host got out whiskey and tumblers and stood a small copper kettle on the fire.

13. At the third glass his eyes got brighter, and he began to talk, the little family circle regarding with eager interest this visitor from distant parts, as he squared his broad shoulders in the chair and spoke of wild scenes and doughty deeds; of wars and plagues and strange peoples.

14. "Twenty-one years of it," said Mr. White, nodding at his wife and son. "When he went away he was a slip of a youth in the warehouse. Now look at him."

15. "He don't look to have taken much harm," said Mrs. White, politely.

16. "I'd like to go to India myself," said the old man, "just to look round a bit, you know."

17. "Better where you are," said the sergeant-major, shaking his head. He put down the empty glass, and sighing softly, shook it again.

18. "I should like to see those old temples and **fakirs** and jugglers," said the old man. "What was that you started telling me the other day about a monkey's paw or something, Morris?"

19. "Nothing," said the soldier, hastily. "Leastways nothing worth hearing."

20. "Monkey's paw?" said Mrs. White, curiously.

21. "Well, it's just a bit of what you might call magic, perhaps," said the sergeant-major, offhandedly.

22. His three listeners leaned forward eagerly. The visitor absent-mindedly put his empty glass to his lips and then set it down again. His host filled it for him.

23. "To look at," said the sergeant-major, fumbling in his pocket, "it's just an ordinary little paw, dried to a mummy."

24 He took something out of his pocket and proffered it. Mrs. White drew back with a grimace, but her son, taking it, examined it curiously.

25 "And what is there special about it?" inquired Mr. White as he took it from his son, and having examined it, placed it upon the table.

26 "It had a spell put on it by an old fakir," said the sergeant-major, "a very holy man. He wanted to show that fate ruled people's lives, and that those who interfered with it did so to their sorrow. He put a spell on it so that three separate men could each have three wishes from it."

27 His manner was so impressive that his hearers were conscious that their light laughter jarred somewhat.

28 "Well, why don't you have three, sir?" said Herbert White, cleverly.

29 The soldier regarded him in the way that middle age is wont to regard presumptuous youth. "I have," he said, quietly, and his blotchy face whitened.

30 "And did you really have the three wishes granted?" asked Mrs. White.

31 "I did," said the sergeant-major, and his glass tapped against his strong teeth.

32 "And has anybody else wished?" persisted the old lady.

33 "The first man had his three wishes. Yes," was the reply; "I don't know what the first two were, but the third was for death. That's how I got the paw."

34 His tones were so grave that a hush fell upon the group.

35 "If you've had your three wishes, it's no good to you now, then, Morris," said the old man at last. "What do you keep it for?"

36 The soldier shook his head. "Fancy, I suppose," he said, slowly. "I did have some idea of selling it, but I don't think I will. It has caused enough mischief already. Besides, people won't buy. They think it's a fairy tale; some of them, and those who do think anything of it want to try it first and pay me afterward."

37 "If you could have another three wishes," said the old man, eyeing him keenly, "would you have them?"

38 "I don't know," said the other. "I don't know."

39 He took the paw, and dangling it between his forefinger and thumb, suddenly threw it upon the fire. White, with a slight cry, stooped down and snatched it off.

40 "Better let it burn," said the soldier, solemnly.

41 "If you don't want it, Morris," said the other, "give it to me."

42 "I won't," said his friend, doggedly. "I threw it on the fire. If you keep it, don't blame me for what happens. Pitch it on the fire again like a sensible man."

43 The other shook his head and examined his new possession closely. "How do you do it?" he inquired.

44 "Hold it up in your right hand and wish aloud," said the sergeant-major, "but I warn you of the **consequences.**"

45 "Sounds like the Arabian Nights," said Mrs. White, as she rose and began to set the supper. "Don't you think you might wish for four pairs of hands for me?"

46 Her husband drew the **talisman** from pocket, and then all three burst into laughter as the sergeant-major, with a look of alarm on his face, caught him by the arm.

47 "If you must wish," he said, gruffly, "wish for something sensible."

48 Mr. White dropped it back in his pocket, and placing chairs, motioned his friend to the table. In the business of supper the talisman was partly forgotten, and afterward the three sat listening in an enthralled fashion to a second installment of the soldier's adventures in India.

49 "If the tale about the monkey's paw is not more truthful than those he has been telling us," said Herbert, as the door closed behind their guest, just in time for him to catch the last train, "we sha'nt make much out of it."

50 "Did you give him anything for it, father?" inquired Mrs. White, regarding her husband closely.

51 "A trifle," said he, colouring slightly. "He didn't want it, but I made him take it. And he pressed me again to throw it away."

52 "Likely," said Herbert, with pretended horror. "Why, we're going to be rich, and famous and happy. Wish to be an emperor, father, to begin with; then you can't be henpecked."

53 He darted round the table, pursued by the maligned Mrs. White armed with an antimacassar.

54 Mr. White took the paw from his pocket and eyed it dubiously. "I don't know what to wish for, and that's a fact," he said, slowly. "It seems to me I've got all I want."

55 "If you only cleared the house, you'd be quite happy, wouldn't you?" said Herbert, with his hand on his shoulder. "Well, wish for two hundred pounds, then; that 'll just do it."

56 His father, smiling shamefacedly at his own credulity, held up the talisman, as his son, with a solemn face, somewhat marred by a wink at his mother, sat down at the piano and struck a few impressive chords.

57 "I wish for two hundred pounds," said the old man distinctly.

58 A fine crash from the piano greeted the words, interrupted by a shuddering cry from the old man. His wife and son ran toward him.

59 "It moved," he cried, with a glance of disgust at the object as it lay on the floor.

60 "As I wished, it twisted in my hand like a snake."

61 "Well, I don't see the money," said his son as he picked it up and placed it on the table, "and I bet I never shall."

62 "It must have been your fancy, father," said his wife, regarding him anxiously.

63 He shook his head. "Never mind, though; there's no harm done, but it gave me a shock all the same."

64 They sat down by the fire again while the two men finished their pipes. Outside, the wind was higher than ever, and the old man started nervously at the sound of a door banging upstairs. A silence unusual and depressing settled upon all three, which lasted until the old couple rose to retire for the night.

65 "I expect you'll find the cash tied up in a big bag in the middle of your bed," said Herbert, as he bade them good-night, "and something horrible squatting up on top of the wardrobe watching you as you pocket your ill-gotten gains."

66 He sat alone in the darkness, gazing at the dying fire, and seeing faces in it. The last face was so horrible and so simian that he gazed at it in amazement. It got so vivid that, with a little uneasy laugh, he felt on the table for a glass containing a little water to throw over it. His hand grasped the monkey's paw, and with a little shiver he wiped his hand on his coat and went up to bed.

II.

67 In the brightness of the wintry sun next morning as it streamed over the breakfast table he laughed at his fears. There was an air of prosaic wholesomeness about the room which it had lacked on the previous night, and the dirty, shrivelled little paw was pitched on the sideboard with a carelessness which betokened no great belief in its virtues.

68 "I suppose all old soldiers are the same," said Mrs. White. "The idea of our listening to such nonsense! How could wishes be granted in these days? And if they could, how could two hundred pounds hurt you, father?"

69 "Might drop on his head from the sky," said the frivolous Herbert.

70 "Morris said the things happened so naturally," said his father, "that you might if you so wished attribute it to coincidence."

71 "Well, don't break into the money before I come back," said Herbert as he rose from the table. "I'm afraid it'll turn you into a mean, avaricious man, and we shall have to disown you."

72 His mother laughed, and following him to the door, watched him down the road; and returning to the breakfast table, was very happy at the expense of her husband's credulity. All of which did not prevent her from scurrying to the door at the postman's knock, nor prevent her from referring somewhat shortly to retired sergeant-majors of bibulous habits when she found that the post brought a tailor's bill.

73 "Herbert will have some more of his funny remarks, I expect, when he comes home," she said, as they sat at dinner.

74 "I dare say," said Mr. White, pouring himself out some beer; "but for all that, the thing moved in my hand; that I'll swear to."

75 "You thought it did," said the old lady soothingly.

76 "I say it did," replied the other. "There was no thought about it; I had just— What's the matter?"

77 His wife made no reply. She was watching the mysterious movements of a man outside, who, peering in an undecided fashion at the house, appeared to be trying to make up his mind to enter. In mental connection with the two hundred pounds, she noticed that the stranger was well dressed, and wore a silk hat of glossy newness. Three times he paused at the gate, and then walked on again. The fourth time he stood with his hand upon it, and then with sudden resolution flung it open and walked up the path. Mrs. White at

the same moment placed her hands behind her, and hurriedly unfastening the strings of her apron, put that useful article of apparel beneath the cushion of her chair.

78 She brought the stranger, who seemed ill at ease, into the room. He gazed at her furtively, and listened in a preoccupied fashion as the old lady apologized for the appearance of the room, and her husband's coat, a garment which he usually reserved for the garden. She then waited as patiently as her sex would permit, for him to broach his business, but he was at first strangely silent.

79 "I—was asked to call," he said at last, and stooped and picked a piece of cotton from his trousers. "I come from 'Maw and Meggins.'"

80 The old lady started. "Is anything the matter?" she asked, breathlessly. "Has anything happened to Herbert? What is it? What is it?"

81 Her husband interposed. "There, there, mother," he said, hastily. "Sit down, and don't jump to conclusions. You've not brought bad news, I'm sure, sir;" and he eyed the other wistfully.

82 "I'm sorry—" began the visitor.

83 "Is he hurt?" demanded the mother, wildly.

84 The visitor bowed in assent. "Badly hurt," he said, quietly, "but he is not in any pain."

85 "Oh, thank God!" said the old woman, clasping her hands. "Thank God for that! Thank—"

86 She broke off suddenly as the sinister meaning of the assurance dawned upon her and she saw the awful confirmation of her fears in the other's averted face. She caught her breath, and turning to her slower-witted husband, laid her trembling old hand upon his. There was a long silence.

87 "He was caught in the machinery," said the visitor at length in a low voice.

88 "Caught in the machinery," repeated Mr. White, in a dazed fashion, "yes."

89 He sat staring blankly out at the window, and taking his wife's hand between his own, pressed it as he had been wont to do in their old courting-days nearly forty years before.

90 "He was the only one left to us," he said, turning gently to the visitor. "It is hard."

91 The other coughed, and rising, walked slowly to the window. "The firm wished me to convey their sincere sympathy with you in your great loss," he said, without looking round. "I beg that you will understand I am only their servant and merely obeying orders."

92 There was no reply; the old woman's face was white, her eyes staring, and her breath inaudible; on the husband's face was a look such as his friend the sergeant might have carried into his first action.

93 "I was to say that 'Maw and Meggins' disclaim all responsibility," continued the other. "They admit no liability at all, but in consideration of your son's services, they wish to present you with a certain sum as compensation."

94 Mr. White dropped his wife's hand, and rising to his feet, gazed with a look of horror at his visitor. His dry lips shaped the words, "How much?"

95 "Two hundred pounds," was the answer.

96 Unconscious of his wife's shriek, the old man smiled faintly, put out his hands like a sightless man, and dropped, a senseless heap, to the floor.

III.

97 In the huge new cemetery, some two miles distant, the old people buried their dead, and came back to a house steeped in shadow and silence. It was all over so quickly that at first they could hardly realize it, and remained in a state of expectation as though of something else to happen—something else which was to lighten this load, too heavy for old hearts to bear.

98 But the days passed, and expectation gave place to **resignation**—the hopeless resignation of the old, sometimes miscalled, apathy. Sometimes they hardly exchanged a word, for now they had nothing to talk about, and their days were long to weariness.

99 It was about a week after that the old man, waking suddenly in the night, stretched out his hand and found himself alone. The room was in darkness, and the sound of subdued weeping came from the window. He raised himself in bed and listened.

100 "Come back," he said, tenderly. "You will be cold."

101 "It is colder for my son," said the old woman, and wept afresh.

102 The sound of her sobs died away on his ears. The bed was warm, and his eyes heavy with sleep. He dozed fitfully, and then slept until a sudden wild cry from his wife awoke him with a start.

STUDYSYNC LIBRARY | The Monkey's Paw

NOTES

103 "The paw!" she cried wildly. "The monkey's paw!"

104 He started up in alarm. "Where? Where is it? What's the matter?"

105 She came stumbling across the room toward him. "I want it," she said, quietly. "You've not destroyed it?"

106 "It's in the parlour, on the bracket," he replied, marvelling. "Why?"

107 She cried and laughed together, and bending over, kissed his cheek.

108 "I only just thought of it," she said, hysterically. "Why didn't I think of it before? Why didn't you think of it?"

109 "Think of what?" he questioned.

110 "The other two wishes," she replied, rapidly. "We've only had one."

111 "Was not that enough?" he demanded, fiercely.

112 "No," she cried, triumphantly; "we'll have one more. Go down and get it quickly, and wish our boy alive again."

113 The man sat up in bed and flung the bedclothes from his quaking limbs. "Good God, you are mad!" he cried, aghast.

114 "Get it," she panted; "get it quickly, and wish—Oh, my boy, my boy!"

115 Her husband struck a match and lit the candle. "Get back to bed," he said, unsteadily. "You don't know what you are saying."

116 "We had the first wish granted," said the old woman, feverishly; "why not the second?"

117 "A coincidence," stammered the old man.

118 "Go and get it and wish," cried his wife, quivering with excitement.

119 The old man turned and regarded her, and his voice shook. "He has been dead ten days, and besides he—I would not tell you else, but—I could only recognize him by his clothing. If he was too terrible for you to see then, how now?"

120 "Bring him back," cried the old woman, and dragged him toward the door. "Do you think I fear the child I have nursed?"

121 He went down in the darkness, and felt his way to the parlour, and then to the mantelpiece. The talisman was in its place, and a horrible fear that the unspoken wish might bring his mutilated son before him ere he could escape

from the room seized upon him, and he caught his breath as he found that he had lost the direction of the door. His brow cold with sweat, he felt his way round the table, and groped along the wall until he found himself in the small passage with the unwholesome thing in his hand.

122 Even his wife's face seemed changed as he entered the room. It was white and expectant, and to his fears seemed to have an unnatural look upon it. He was afraid of her.

123 "Wish!" she cried, in a strong voice.

124 "It is foolish and wicked," he faltered.

125 "Wish!" repeated his wife.

126 He raised his hand. "I wish my son alive again."

127 The talisman fell to the floor, and he regarded it fearfully. Then he sank trembling into a chair as the old woman, with burning eyes, walked to the window and raised the blind.

128 He sat until he was chilled with the cold, glancing occasionally at the figure of the old woman peering through the window. The candle-end, which had burned below the rim of the china candlestick, was throwing pulsating shadows on the ceiling and walls, until, with a flicker larger than the rest, it expired. The old man, with an unspeakable sense of relief at the failure of the talisman, crept back to his bed, and a minute or two afterward the old woman came silently and apathetically beside him.

129 Neither spoke, but lay silently listening to the ticking of the clock. A stair creaked, and a squeaky mouse scurried noisily through the wall. The darkness was oppressive, and after lying for some time screwing up his courage, he took the box of matches, and striking one, went downstairs for a candle.

130 At the foot of the stairs the match went out, and he paused to strike another; and at the same moment a knock, so quiet and stealthy as to be scarcely audible, sounded on the front door.

131 The matches fell from his hand and spilled in the passage. He stood motionless, his breath suspended until the knock was repeated. Then he turned and fled swiftly back to his room, and closed the door behind him. A third knock sounded through the house.

132 "What's that?" cried the old woman, starting up.

133 "A rat," said the old man in shaking tones—"a rat. It passed me on the stairs."

134 His wife sat up in bed listening. A loud knock resounded through the house.

135 "It's Herbert!" she screamed. "It's Herbert!"

136 She ran to the door, but her husband was before her, and catching her by the arm, held her tightly.

137 "What are you going to do?" he whispered hoarsely.

138 "It's my boy; it's Herbert!" she cried, struggling mechanically. "I forgot it was two miles away. What are you holding me for? Let go. I must open the door."

139 "For God's sake don't let it in," cried the old man, trembling.

140 "You're afraid of your own son," she cried, struggling. "Let me go. I'm coming, Herbert; I'm coming."

141 There was another knock, and another. The old woman with a sudden wrench broke free and ran from the room. Her husband followed to the landing, and called after her appealingly as she hurried downstairs. He heard the chain rattle back and the bottom bolt drawn slowly and stiffly from the socket. Then the old woman's voice, strained and panting.

142 "The bolt," she cried, loudly. "Come down. I can't reach it."

143 But her husband was on his hands and knees groping wildly on the floor in search of the paw. If he could only find it before the thing outside got in. A perfect fusillade of knocks reverberated through the house, and he heard the scraping of a chair as his wife put it down in the passage against the door. He heard the creaking of the bolt as it came slowly back, and at the same moment he found the monkey's paw, and frantically breathed his third and last wish.

144 The knocking ceased suddenly, although the echoes of it were still in the house. He heard the chair drawn back, and the door opened. A cold wind rushed up the staircase, and a long loud wail of disappointment and misery from his wife gave him courage to run down to her side, and then to the gate beyond. The street lamp flickering opposite shone on a quiet and deserted road.

THINK QUESTIONS

1. What is "the monkey's paw"? What is Herbert White's attitude toward the monkey's paw? Cite textual evidence from the selection to support your answer.

2. Foreshadowing is a literary device in which a writer gives an advance hint of what is to come later in the story. How does the author of "The Monkey's Paw" use foreshadowing in the first chapter to suggest that the spell placed on the paw might not bring happiness to whomever possesses it? Cite textual evidence from the selection to support your answer.

3. Compare Mr. White's feelings about the monkey's paw when he makes the first wish, second wish, and third wish. How does his attitude change? Cite textual evidence from the selection to support your answer.

4. Use context to determine the meaning of the word **fakirs** as it is used in paragraph 18 of "The Monkey's Paw." The singular form is used in paragraph 26. Write your definition of "fakirs" and explain how you figured it out. How can you check the word's precise meaning as well as its pronunciation?

5. Find the word **consequences** in paragraph 44. Use context clues in the surrounding sentences, as well as the sentence in which *consequences* appears, to determine the word's meaning. Write your definition of "consequences" and explain how you figured it out. Then check the meaning in a dictionary.

STUDYSYNC LIBRARY | The Monkey's Paw

CLOSE READ

Reread the short story "The Monkey's Paw." As you reread, complete the Focus Questions below. Then use your answers and annotations from the questions to help you complete the Writing Prompt.

FOCUS QUESTIONS

1. How does Mr. White approach the game of chess that he plays with his son Herbert? What does this reveal about his personality, and how he will react when he learns about the monkey's paw later in the story? Support your answer with textual evidence.

2. How does Mrs. White's attitude, as well as her circumstances, create a problem for both her and Mr. White at the end of the story? How does the setting add to the suspense? Cite textual evidence to support your answer.

3. What causes the downfall of the White family, and how is it related to the theme of "The Monkey's Paw"? Cite textual evidence to support your answer.

4. The entire story is set in the Whites' home, yet it seems different in each of the three parts of the story. Why are these changes significant? How do they contribute to the theme of the story? Highlight evidence to support your ideas and write annotations to explain your choices.

5. What elements of "The Monkey's Paw" might attract people to this story? Cite textual evidence from the selection to support your answer.

WRITING PROMPT

How do the story elements of character, setting, and plot contribute to the theme of "The Monkey's Paw"? Use your understanding of story elements to determine the theme of the short story. Then discuss how the elements combine to contribute to that theme. Support your writing with evidence from the text.

SORRY, WRONG NUMBER

DRAMA
Lucille Fletcher
1948

INTRODUCTION

Lucille Fletcher's play from the 1940s (famously produced for radio audiences only as well) relies on voices and sound effects to create a world of increasing fear for a neurotic woman alone in her New York apartment. The excerpt is from the opening scene.

STUDYSYNC LIBRARY | Sorry, Wrong Number

"Make it quick. As little blood as possible."

 FIRST READ

EXCERPT FROM ACT ONE

1 [SCENE: *As curtain rises, we see a divided stage, only the center part of which is lighted and furnished as* MRS. STEVENSON'S *bedroom. Expensive, rather **fussy** furnishings. A large bed, on which* MRS. STEVENSON, *clad in bed jacket, is lying. A night-table close by, with phone, lighted lamp, and pill bottles. A mantle, with clock, right. A closed door, right. A window, with curtains closed, rear. The set is lit by one lamp on a night-table. It is enclosed by three flats. Beyond this central set, the stage, on either side, is in darkness.*]

2 MRS. STEVENSON *is dialing a number on the phone, as curtain rises. She listens to phone, slams down receiver in irritation. As she does so, we hear sound of a train roaring by in the distance. She reaches for her pill bottle, pours herself a glass of water, shakes out pill, swallows it, then reaches for the phone again, dials number nervously.*]

3 [SOUND: *Number being dialed on phone: Busy signal.*]

4 MRS. STEVENSON [*a **querulous**, self-centered **neurotic***]: Oh—dear! [*Slams down receiver, dials* OPERATOR.]

5 [SCENE: *A spotlight, left of side flat, picks up out of **peripheral** darkness, figure of* 1st OPERATOR, *sitting with headphones at small table. If spotlight not available, use flashlight, clicked on by* 1st OPERATOR, *illuminating her face.*]

6 OPERATOR: Your call, please?

7 MRS. STEVENSON: Operator? I've been dialing Murray Hill 4-0098 now for the last three-quarters of an hour, and the line is always busy. But I don't see how it *could* be busy that long. Will you try it for me please?

8 OPERATOR: Murray Hill 4-0098? One moment, please.

9 [SCENE: *She makes gesture of plugging in call through switchboard.*]

10 MRS. STEVENSON: I don't see how it could be busy all this time. It's my husband's office. He's working late tonight, and I'm all alone here in this house. My health is very poor—and I've been feeling so nervous all day—

11 OPERATOR: Ringing Murray Hill 4-0098.

12 [SOUND: *Phone buzz. It rings three times. Receiver is picked up at other end.*]

13 MAN: Hello.

14 MRS. STEVENSON: Hello? *[A little puzzled.]* Hello. Is Mr. Stevenson there?

15 MAN *[into phone, as though he had not heard]*: Hello. *[Louder.]* Hello.

16 SECOND MAN *[slow, heavy quality, faintly foreign accent]*: Hello.

17 FIRST MAN: Hello. George?

18 GEORGE: Yes, sir.

19 MRS. STEVENSON *[louder and more **imperious,** to phone]*: Hello. Who's this? What number am I calling, please?

20 FIRST MAN: We have heard from our client. He says the coast is clear for tonight.

21 GEORGE: Yes, sir.

22 FIRST MAN: Where are you now?

23 GEORGE: In a phone booth.

24 FIRST MAN: Okay. You know the address. At eleven o'clock the private patrolman goes around to the bar on Second Avenue for a beer. Be sure that all the lights downstairs are out. There should be only one light visible from the street. At eleven fifteen a subway train crosses the bridge. It makes a noise in case her window is open and she should scream.

25 MRS. STEVENSON [shocked]: Oh—*hello!* What number is this, please?

26 GEORGE: Okay. I understand.

27 FIRST MAN: Make it quick. As little blood as possible. Our client does not wish to make her suffer long.

28 GEORGE: A knife okay, sir?

29 FIRST MAN: Yes. A knife will be okay. And remember—remove the rings and bracelets, and the jewelry in the bureau drawer. Our client wishes it to look like a simple robbery.

30 [SOUND: *A bland buzzing signal.*]

31 MRS. STEVENSON [*clicking phone*]: Oh! [*Bland buzzing signal continues. She hangs up.*] How awful! How unspeakably—

Excerpted from *Sorry, Wrong Number* by Lucille Fletcher, published by Dramatists Play Service, Inc.

THINK QUESTIONS

1. How is Mrs. Stevenson feeling as the scene begins? How do we know she is feeling that way? Cite details from the text to explain her condition.

2. How does the setting help emphasize that Mrs. Stevenson is alone? Cite evidence from the stage directions to explain.

3. Why do you think Mrs. Stevenson explains her health condition to the operator? Use textual evidence to explain your inference.

4. Use context to determine the meaning of the word **imperious** as it is used in paragraph 19 of "Sorry, Wrong Number." Write your definition of "imperious" and explain how you figured it out.

5. Knowing that the Greek prefix *peri-* means "about" or "around," you can use this knowledge and context to help you determine the meaning of **peripheral** in paragraph 5. Write your definition of peripheral and explain how you figured it out.

CLOSE READ

Reread the short drama "Sorry, Wrong Number." As you reread, complete the Focus Questions below. Then use your answers and annotations from the questions to help you complete the Writing Prompt.

FOCUS QUESTIONS

1. How do Mrs. Stevenson's character traits affect the plot of the play? What can you infer about her situation based on her short exchange with the telephone operator? Cite specific evidence from the text in your response.

2. From the information the author provides about the setting, and the details she reveals about the murder plot Mrs. Stevenson overhears, what inferences can you make that suggest Mrs. Stevenson herself might be the intended victim? Support your answer with evidence from the text.

3. How does the author use the stage directions in the play to reveal aspects of Mrs. Stevenson's character? Cite text evidence to support your answer.

4. Use your understanding of plot development to help you summarize the exposition of the drama. Highlight evidence from the text that will help support your answer.

5. Mrs. Stevenson cannot be heard by the other callers, and she slowly realizes that she is hearing something she obviously was not intended to hear. Highlight the part of the text where Mrs. Stevenson and the reader know for sure that the callers are planning a crime. What draws the reader into the story's suspense?

WRITING PROMPT

Analyze the ways in which fear and suspense is introduced and maintained during this play's developing plot. Consider how the suspense naturally causes the reader to make predictions about what may happen in the text. Consider the sound effects, the content and structure of the lines, and the way the characters' voices may sound when the lines are spoken aloud on a stage. Use textual evidence from *Sorry, Wrong Number* to support your analysis.

VIOLENCE IN THE MOVIES

NON-FICTION
2014

INTRODUCTION

In these two articles the writers make arguments for and against the use of violence in the movies. This debate has been going on since people began to gather together to watch cinematic performances like "The Great Train Robbery" in 1903. Both writers present strong arguments and support their claims with evidence. Which of the writers does the better job in convincing you that his or her view is correct?

"The typical American child will view more than 200,000 acts of violence…"

FIRST READ

1   **Violence in the Movies: Cinematic Craft or Hollywood Gone Too Far?**

2   **Point:** Hollywood, Stop Exposing Our Kids to Violence!

3   Violence in Hollywood movies has become excessive and is putting our youth and our entire society at risk for violent behaviors. In the golden age of Hollywood, filmmakers relied on solid storytelling techniques to entertain audiences. Unfortunately, today's film industry often draws audiences to movie theaters with promotional promises of action-packed violence, brutal murders, and mass destruction.

4   Violence in movies is on the rise. A recent study published by researchers at the Annenberg Public Policy Center (APPC) of the University of Pennsylvania found that "the amount of gun violence shown in PG-13 films has more than tripled since 1985." Children are being exposed to high levels of violence in movies, television, and other media throughout the span of childhood. According to media violence research published by the American Academy of Child and Adolescent Psychiatry, "The typical American child will view more than 200,000 acts of violence, including more than 16,000 murders, before age 18."

5   Researchers have found tremendous evidence supporting a link between exposure to violence in media and violent behavior in children. In 2000, researchers from six leading professional medical organizations, including the American Medical Association and the American Psychiatric Association, reviewed hundreds of scholarly studies on media violence and its influence on **aggressive** behavior in children. They reported their conclusions to Congress, stating that "viewing entertainment violence can lead to increases in aggressive attitudes, values, and behavior, particularly in children."

6 Another 2005 review of such studies, published by *The Lancet* and reported by the *New York Times,* found that "exposure to media violence leads to aggression, **desensitization** toward violence and lack of sympathy for victims of violence, particularly in children." How can anyone deny the existence of a link between media violence and violent behavior in children when it is being proven and supported by our country's top researchers? "The evidence is overwhelming," stated Jeffrey McIntyre of the American Psychological Association. "To argue against it is like arguing against gravity."

7 What Hollywood filmmakers must understand is that children model what they see in movies. When a hero exhibits violent behaviors to defeat an enemy, children learn that violence is an acceptable form of problem solving and conflict resolution. Those who see themselves as victims may be more likely to act out in violent behaviors, whether against peers, parents, teachers, or other authority figures. According to the U.S. Bureau of Justice Statistics, in 2011, students ages 12-18 were victims of 597,500 violent victimizations at school.

8 "Violence in the media has been increasing and reaching proportions that are dangerous," Emanuel Tanay, MD, former Wayne State University professor and forensic psychiatrist, reported to *Psychiatric Times*. "What we call entertainment is really propaganda for violence. If you manufacture guns, you don't need to advertise, because it is done by our entertainment industry." Do we really want to teach our children that guns and violence are the answers to our problems?

9 Some people do not believe that exposure to violence in movies is a risk factor for violent behavior because they themselves have not been affected by the exposure. However, no one would reasonably argue, "I've always ridden my bicycle without a helmet, and I have never incurred a head injury. Therefore, there is no link between not wearing a bicycle helmet and increasing your risk of getting a head injury." Why apply such flawed reasoning when it comes to violence in Hollywood movies?

10 Others suggest that it is up to parents to protect their children from violence in films by following the rating guidelines set by the Motion Picture Association of America (MPAA). However, APPC researchers report that PG-13 movies portray the same amount of violence as is shown in R-rated movies. Parents can no longer rely on MPAA's film ratings to help determine which movies are suitable for children of different ages.

11 Of course, media violence is not the only risk factor for violent behavior in children, but it is certainly a large threat. Screenwriters and moviemakers do not need to resort to depictions of sensational violence that put children and the society at large at risk in order to entertain audiences. Good storytelling

creates suspense and keeps an audience engaged with the suggestion that something terrible is about to happen. Playwrights of Ancient Greece included violent elements such as murder and suicide in their stories, but these violent actions happened offstage, and audiences remained emotionally engaged just the same. Movies should present scenarios in which conflict is resolved through nonviolent behaviors, without weapons. It's time to hold filmmakers accountable for the violent messages they are sending out to society and to our children.

12 **Counterpoint:** Hollywood Filmmakers Should Not be Villainized for Movie Violence

13 Hollywood filmmakers include violence in movies as part of the craft of storytelling, to create an enjoyable movie-going experience for the audience. It is not right to restrict their abilities to tell stories through film, nor is it right to limit entertainment options for people who enjoy watching action and horror movies and have no tendency toward violence.

14 Some people feel that violence in media causes people to act violently in real life.

15 This just isn't true. I watch violent movies on a regular basis, and I have never engaged in violent behavior. I'm not the only one, either. Millions of Americans see violent imagery in films and on TV every day, but very few commit violent crimes.

16 Violent behavior is an extremely complex issue that cannot be reduced to a simple cause-effect relationship. According to the Center for Disease Control and Prevention (CDC), risk factors for youth violence include history of early aggressive behavior, exposure to violence in the family, low parental involvement, association with delinquent peers, low IQ, poor academic performance, low socioeconomic status, and many others. Exposure to violence in movies does not appear on the CDC's list.

17 Although some psychological studies seem to prove a connection between media violence and violent behavior, those links are not significant enough to justify restrictions on movies. Jonathan L. Freedman, a professor of psychology at the University of Toronto, reported "a very small **correlation**" between media violence and aggressive behavior in children. Freedman suggested that violent behavior is most likely present in children who lack regular adult supervision. How can we hold filmmakers responsible for putting children at risk for violence and aggression when it's a parental duty to monitor what children are watching? Parents must teach their children appropriate behaviors and help their children interpret the violence they encounter in movies as fantasy, not reality.

STUDYSYNC LIBRARY | Violence in the Movies

NOTES

18   Opponents of movie violence claim that crime is on the rise. According to the U.S. Bureau of Justice Statistics, crime rates have dropped steadily since 1993, when 80 of every 1,000 people reported being victims of violent crime. The homicide rate declined 48% from 1993 to 2011. In fact, violent movies may actually play a part in this reduction in violent crime. Children who are watching a movie are taking part in a nonviolent activity. Movie watching provides time for entertainment and takes away from the time in which these children might engage in violent behaviors. According to Gordon Dahl and Stefano DellaVigna, research associates of the National Bureau of Economic Research, "estimates suggest that in the short-run violent movies deter almost 1,000 assaults on an average weekend." Because watching violent movies provides those who might otherwise engage in violent behaviors with an alternative, nonviolent activity, it turns out to be a beneficial activity to those with aggressive tendencies. Do we really want to restrict violence in movies and risk an increase in violent crime?

19   Violence has existed in entertainment for centuries, starting with the epic literature and mythology of ancient civilizations through the sixteenth century esteemed works of William Shakespeare. Yet human societies have actually become less violent over time. The violence we see in movies does not **dictate** how we act toward one another in real life. It exists as a storytelling tool to engage an audience, much like the tools of suspense and humor, and is an effective aid to teach morality through stories of good and evil. We must leave filmmakers to their artistry and allow them to contribute to our culture without censoring their craft.

THINK QUESTIONS

1. What is the author's position about violence in the movies in the Point selection, "Hollywood, Stop Exposing Our Kids to Violence!"? Cite textual evidence to explain your understanding.

2. Why does the author of the Point text include a quote from Jeffrey McIntyre in paragraph 4? Cite an example from the text to explain your answer.

3. How does the author of the Counterpoint text, "Hollywood Filmmakers Should Not Be Villainized for Movie Violence," respond to the first author's viewpoint?

4. The author of the second passage writes that one professor reported "'a very small **correlation**' between media violence and aggressive behavior in children." Remember that the Latin prefix *co-* means "together with." Use your knowledge of the prefix along with context clues to determine the meaning of the word "correlation." Write the definition and explain how you figured it out.

5. Use a print or online dictionary to determine the meaning of the word **aggressive**. Write your definition of "aggressive," along with its part of speech, and tell how you figured out the meaning.

STUDYSYNC LIBRARY | Violence in the Movies

CLOSE READ

Reread the debate about violence in the movies. As you reread, complete the Focus Questions below. Then use your answers and annotations from the questions to help you complete the Writing Prompt.

FOCUS QUESTIONS

1. In paragraph 2 of the article, the author states, "Children are being exposed to high levels of violence in movies, television, and other media throughout the span of childhood." What textual evidence does the author give to support this point of view?

2. In the eleventh and twelfth paragraphs of the article, the author states, "Some people feel that violence in media causes people to act violently in real life. This just isn't true. I watch violent movies on a regular basis, and I have never engaged in violent behavior." Does this statement alone provide strong support for the author's point of view? Why or why not? What factual evidence does the author present to back up this statement?

3. In both the "Point" and "Counterpoint" sections of the article, the authors cite entertainment created hundreds and even thousands of years ago in order to support their specific points of view. How does each author make use of these older forms of entertainments in the article as supporting evidence? Which do you think is more successful? Cite textual evidence to support your answer.

4. The authors often ask questions of the reader in both the "Point" and "Counterpoint" sections of the article, knowing that readers will not be able to answer them directly. Why might an author choose to express a point of view in the form of a question? Highlight the question the author asks in the fourth paragraph of the "Point" section. Then make annotations rewriting the question in the form of a statement expressing the author's point of view.

5. How do you think the author of the second article might answer the question "What attracts people to stories of suspense?" Use details and evidence from the text to support your answer.

WRITING PROMPT

The authors of these articles hold different points of view on whether or not violence in Hollywood movies has a negative effect on society. Which author is more convincing? Which author best supports his or her points with strong evidence? Use your understanding of point of view and supporting evidence to defend one of the two claims. Support your writing with evidence from the text and additional media evidence support.

A NIGHT TO REMEMBER

NON-FICTION
Walter Lord
1955

INTRODUCTION

Walter Lord interviewed scores of *Titanic* survivors to create a powerful account of the ship's sinking in the calm, frigid North Atlantic on April 14, 1912. In this passage, we hear a variety of reactions at the beginning of the disaster, from the first sighting of an iceberg by the ship's lookout to the mysterious jolt heard and felt by crew members and passengers alike, each observer interpreting the impact differently.

"He felt sure the ship had struck something but he didn't know what."

FIRST READ

From Chapter: "Another Belfast Trip"

1. High in the crow's-nest of the New White Star Liner *Titanic,* Lookout Frederick Fleet peered into a dazzling night. It was calm, clear and bitterly cold. There was no moon, but the cloudless sky blazed with stars. The Atlantic was like polished plate glass; people later said they had never seen it so smooth.

2. This was the fifth night of the *Titanic's* maiden voyage to New York, and it was already clear that she was not only the largest but also the most glamorous ship in the world. Even the passengers' dogs were glamorous. John Jacob Astor had along his Airedale Kitty. Henry Sleeper Harper, of the publishing family, had his prize Pekingese Sun Yat-sen. Robert W. Daniel, the Philadelphia banker, was bringing back a champion French bulldog just purchased in Britain. Clarence Moore of Washington also had been dog-shopping, but the 50 pairs of English foxhounds he bought for the Loudoun Hunt weren't making the trip.

3. That was all another world to Frederick Fleet. He was one of six lookouts carried by the *Titanic,* and the lookouts didn't worry about passenger problems. They were the "eyes of the ship," and on this particular night Fleet had been warned to watch especially for icebergs.

4. So far, so good. On duty at 10 o'clock . . . a few words about the ice problem with Lookout Reginald Lee, who shared the same watch . . . a few more words about the cold … but mostly just silence, as the two men stared into the darkness.

5. Now the watch was almost over, and still there was nothing unusual. Just the night, the stars, the biting cold, the wind that whistled through the rigging as the *Titanic* raced across the calm, black sea at 22 1/2 knots. It was almost 11:40 P.M. on Sunday, the 14th of April, 1912.

6. Suddenly Fleet saw something directly ahead, even darker than the darkness. At first it was small (about the size, he thought, of two tables put together), but every second it grew larger and closer. Quickly Fleet banged the crow's-nest bell three times, the warning of danger ahead. At the same time he lifted the phone and rang the bridge.

7. "What did you see?" asked a calm voice at the other end.

8. "Iceberg right ahead," replied Fleet.

9. "Thank you," acknowledged the voice with curiously **detached** courtesy. Nothing more was said.

10. For the next 37 seconds, Fleet and Lee stood quietly side by side, watching the ice draw nearer. Now they were almost on top of it, and still the ship didn't turn. The berg towered wet and glistening far above the forecastle deck, and both men braced themselves for a crash. Then, miraculously, the bow began to swing to port. At the last second the stem shot into the clear, and the ice glided swiftly by along the starboard side. It looked to Fleet like a very close shave.

11. At this moment Quartermaster George Thomas Rowe was standing watch on the after bridge. For him too, it had been an uneventful night—just the sea, the stars, the biting cold. As he paced the deck, he noticed what he and his mates called "Whiskers 'round the Light"—tiny splinters of ice in the air, fine as dust, that gave off **myriads** of bright colors whenever caught in the glow of the deck lights.

12. Then suddenly he felt a curious motion break the steady rhythm of the engines. It was a little like coming alongside a dock wall rather heavily. He glanced forward—and stared again. A windjammer, sails set, seemed to be passing along the starboard side. Then he realized it was an iceberg, towering perhaps 100 feet above the water. The next instant it was gone, drifting astern into the dark.

13. Meanwhile, down below in the First Class dining saloon on D Deck, four other members of the *Titanic's* crew were sitting around one of the tables. The last diner had long since departed, and now the big white Jacobean room was empty except for this single group. They were dining-saloon **stewards,** indulging in the time-honored pastime of all stewards off duty—they were gossiping about their passengers.

14. Then, as they sat there talking, a faint grinding jar seemed to come from somewhere deep inside the ship. It was not much, but enough to break the conversation and rattle the silver that was set for breakfast next morning.

15. Steward James Johnson felt he knew just what it was. He recognized the kind of shudder a ship gives when she drops a propeller blade, and he knew this sort of mishap meant a trip back to the Harland & Wolff Shipyard at Belfast—with plenty of free time to enjoy the hospitality of the port.

16. Somebody near him agreed and sang out cheerfully, "Another Belfast trip!"

17. In the galley just to the stern, Chief Night Baker Walter Belford was making rolls for the following day. (The honor of baking fancy pastry was reserved for the day shift.) When the jolt came, it impressed Belford more strongly than Steward Johnson—perhaps because a pan of new rolls clattered off the top of the oven and scattered about the floor.

18. The passengers in their cabins felt the jar too, and tried to connect it with something familiar. Marguerite Frolicher, a young Swiss girl accompanying her father on a business trip, woke up with a start. Half-asleep, she could think only of the little white lake ferries at Zurich making a sloppy landing. Softly she said to herself, "Isn't it funny ... we're landing!"

19. Major Arthur Godfrey Peuchen, starting to undress for the night, thought it was like a heavy wave striking the ship. Mrs. J. Stuart White was sitting on the edge of her bed, just reaching to turn out the light, when the ship seemed to roll over "a thousand marbles." To Lady Cosmo Duff Gordon, waking up from the jolt, it seemed "as though somebody had drawn a giant finger along the side of the ship." Mrs. John Jacob Astor thought it was some mishap in the kitchen.

20. It seemed stronger to some than to others. Mrs. Albert Caldwell pictured a large dog that had a baby kitten in its mouth and was shaking it. Mrs. Walter B. Stephenson recalled the first **ominous** jolt when she was in the San Francisco earthquake—then decided this wasn't that bad. Mrs. E. D. Appleton felt hardly any shock at all, but she noticed an unpleasant ripping sound ... like someone tearing a long, long strip of **calico.**

21. The jar meant more to J. Bruce Ismay, Managing Director of the White Star Line, who in a festive mood was going along for the ride on the *Titanic's* first trip. Ismay woke up with a start in his deluxe suite on B Deck—he felt sure the ship had struck something, but he didn't know what.

Excerpted from *A Night to Remember* by Walter Lord, published by Bantam Books.

STUDYSYNC LIBRARY | **A Night to Remember**

THINK QUESTIONS

1. The author states that it was clear the *Titanic* was "the most glamorous ship in the world." What made the ship so glamorous? Cite evidence from the text to support your answer.

2. How do various people on board experience the impact of the iceberg? Why does Walter Lord, in this chapter, show how different people on board the *Titanic* experience the impact? Cite textual evidence to support your inference.

3. What were some of the fundamental, or main, differences between crew members and their various jobs on the *Titanic*? Why do you think Lord includes these descriptions? Cite textual evidence to explain your inference.

4. Use context to determine the meaning of the word **myriads** as it is used in paragraph 11 of *A Night to Remember*. Write your definition of "myriads" and tell how you arrived at it.

5. Use context to determine the meaning of the word **stewards** as it is used in paragraph 13 of *A Night to Remember*. Write your definition of "stewards" and tell how you found it. Finally, follow up by consulting a dictionary to clarify the precise meaning of the word.

thud, as if someone had swung a chunk of stovewood against the side of the car. The dog's barking roars of rage were cut off cleanly, and there was silence.

21. *Knocked himself out,* she thought hysterically. *Thank God, thank God for that—*

22. And a moment later Cujo's foam-covered, twisted face popped up outside her window, only inches away, like a horror-movie monster that has decided to give the audience the ultimate thrill by coming right out of the screen. She could see his huge, heavy teeth. And again there was that swooning, terrible feeling that the dog was looking at *her,* not at a woman who just happened to be trapped in her car with her little boy, but at *Donna Trenton,* as if he had just been hanging around, waiting for her to show up.

23. Cujo began to bark again, the sound incredibly loud even through the Saf-T-Glas. And suddenly it occurred to her that if she had not automatically rolled her window up as she brought the Pinto to a stop (something her father had insisted on: stop the car, roll up the windows, set the brake, take the keys, lock the car), she would now be minus her throat. Her blood would be on the wheel, the dash, the windshield. That one action, so automatic she could not even really remember performing it.

24. She screamed.

25. The dog's terrible face dropped from view.

26. She remembered Tad and looked around. When she saw him, a new fear invaded her, drilling like a hot needle. He had not fainted, but he was not really conscious, either. He had fallen back against the seat, his eyes dazed and blank. His face was white. His lips had gone bluish at the corners.

27. "Tad!" She snapped her fingers under his nose, and he blinked sluggishly at the dry sound. "Tad!"

28. "Mommy," he said thickly. "How did the monster in my closet get out? Is it a dream? Is it my nap?"

29. "It's going to be all right," she said, chilled by what he had said about his closet nonetheless. "It's—"

30. She saw the dog's tail and the top of its broad back over the hood of the Pinto. It was going around to Tad's side of the car—

31. And Tad's window wasn't shut.

STUDYSYNC LIBRARY | Cujo

32 She jackknifed across Tad's lap, moving with such a hard muscular spasm that she cracked her fingers on the window crank. She turned it as fast as she could, panting, feeling Tad squirming beneath her.

33 It was three quarters of the way up when Cujo leaped at the window. His muzzle shot in through the closing gap and was forced upward toward the ceiling by the closing window. The sound of his snarling barks filled the small car. Tad shrieked again and wrapped his arms around his head, his forearms crossed over his eyes. He tried to dig his face into Donna's belly, reducing her leverage on the window crank in his blind efforts to get away.

34 "Momma! Momma! Momma! *Make it stop! Make it go away!*"

35 Something warm was running across the backs of her hands. She saw with mounting horror that it was mixed slime and blood running from the dog's mouth. Using everything that she had, she managed to force the window crank through another quarter turn . . . and then Cujo pulled back. She caught just a glimpse of the Saint Bernard's features, twisted and crazy, a mad **caricature** of a friendly Saint Bernard's face. Then it dropped back to all fours and she could only see its back.

36 Now the crank turned easily. She shut the window, then wiped the backs of her hands on her jeans, uttering small cries of **revulsion.**

Excerpted from *Cujo* by Stephen King, published by Signet.

THINK QUESTIONS

1. Based on the descriptions and events in this excerpt, what can you infer about the title character, Cujo? Use textual evidence to explain your inferences.

2. Think about how Donna handles this situation with Cujo. What do Donna's actions and thoughts reveal about her character? Give examples from the text to support your thinking.

3. What is one way the author increases the sense of horror and suspense in this excerpt? Cite textual evidence to explain your ideas.

4. What words in the excerpt help you understand the meaning of the word **languidly** in paragraph 14? Explain the context clues and then write your definition of "languidly."

5. Read this passage from the text: "She caught just a glimpse of the Saint Bernard's features, twisted and crazy, a mad caricature of a friendly Saint Bernard's face." What can you infer about meaning of the word **caricature** in this passage? Write the definition based on the context, and then verify your inferred meaning by using a print or online dictionary.

CLOSE READ

Reread the excerpt from *Cujo*. As you reread, complete the Focus Questions below. Then use your answers and annotations from the questions to help you complete the Writing Prompt.

FOCUS QUESTIONS

1. In the paragraph 24, after all Donna has been through—hearing the dog growl, catching her first glimpse of Cujo's blood soaked fur, getting into the car and securing the door—Stephen King writes simply that "she screamed." Use text evidence to explain why Donna finally lets loose with this expression of terror, even though she is now in relative safety inside the car.

2. At several points in the passage, the author describes how Donna hurts herself. At one point, for example, she hits her leg on the car's fender. Reread the text that describes each of these details. What inference can you make about Donna from this text evidence? How does Stephen King use these incidents to build suspense? Highlight your evidence and annotate to explain your ideas.

3. The characters in this excerpt are Donna Trenton and her son Tad. Readers experience both of them reacting to a frightening situation. What details does the author, Stephen King, include that describe Tad's reaction to the dog? What can you infer about Tad and his fears? Highlight evidence to support your ideas, and write annotations to explain your assessment.

4. What inferences can you make about the situation at the end of the passage? Can you use these inferences to predict what will happen next in the story? Highlight evidence from the text that will help support your prediction.

5. What details hold the reader's attention, creating suspense in the story? Use details from the selection to describe why people are attracted to stories of suspense.

WRITING PROMPT

Ask your teacher for the link needed to view a movie clip. Then respond to the prompt.
Watch the 1983 film version of this scene. Then reread the excerpt. How did director Lewis Teague stay true to the original novel? What liberties did he take with the script? What inferences did you make in the text passage that are retained or abandoned in the film version? In about 300 words, analyze the choices the film director made and the effects these changes have on your perception of the characters as well as the film's level of suspense.

LORD OF THE FLIES

FICTION
William Golding
1954

INTRODUCTION

studysync

When a plane carrying British schoolboys crash-lands on a remote island, the youths' attempt to govern themselves turns into an increasingly brutal struggle for power in William Golding's *Lord of the Flies*. Golding served in the Royal Navy during World War II, and claimed his depiction of the boys' behavior was influenced by his experiences watching how men reacted in the heat of battle. In this excerpt from early in the novel, a group of choir boys has followed the sound of a conch shell to a second group. After a wary sorting out, they decide to elect a leader.

"Seems to me we ought to have a chief to decide things."

 ## FIRST READ

From Chapter 1

1. "Isn't there a ship, then?"

2. Inside the floating cloak he was tall, thin, and bony; and his hair was red beneath the black cap. His face was crumpled and freckled, and ugly without silliness. Out of this face stared two light blue eyes, frustrated now, and turning, or ready to turn, to anger.

3. "Isn't there a man here?"

4. Ralph spoke to his back.

5. "No. We're having a meeting. Come and join in."

6. The group of cloaked boys began to scatter from close line. The tall boy shouted at them.

7. "Choir! Stand still!"

8. Wearily obedient, the choir huddled into line and stood there swaying in the sun. None the less, some began to protest faintly.

9. "But, Merridew. Please, Merridew . . . can't we?"

10. Then one of the boys flopped on his face in the sand and the line broke up. They heaved the fallen boy to the platform and let him lie. Merridew, his eyes staring, made the best of a bad job.

11. "All right then. Sit down. Let him alone."

12. "But Merridew."

13 "He's always throwing a faint," said Merridew. "He did in Gib.; and Addis; and at **matins** over the precentor."

14 This last piece of shop brought sniggers from the choir, who perched like black birds on the criss-cross trunks and examined Ralph with interest. Piggy asked no names. He was intimidated by this uniformed superiority and the offhand authority in Merridew's voice. He shrank to the other side of Ralph and busied himself with his glasses.

15 Merridew turned to Ralph.

16 "Aren't there any grownups?"

17 "No."

18 Merridew sat down on a trunk and looked round the circle.

19 "Then we'll have to look after ourselves."

20 Secure on the other side of Ralph, Piggy spoke timidly.

21 "That's why Ralph made a meeting. So as we can decide what to do. We've heard names. That's Johnny. Those two—they're twins, Sam 'n Eric. Which is Eric—? You? No—you're Sam—"

22 "I'm Sam—"

23 "'n I'm Eric."

24 "We'd better all have names," said Ralph, "so I'm Ralph."

25 "We got most names," said Piggy. "Got 'em just now."

26 "Kids' names," said Merridew. "Why should I be Jack? I'm Merridew."

27 Ralph turned to him quickly. This was the voice of one who knew his own mind.

28 "Then," went on Piggy, "that boy—I forget—"

29 "You're talking too much," said Jack Merridew. "Shut up, Fatty."

30 Laughter arose.

31 "He's not Fatty," cried Ralph, "his real name's Piggy!"

32 "Piggy!"

33 "Piggy!"

34 "Oh, Piggy!"

35 A storm of laughter arose and even the tiniest child joined in. For the moment the boys were a closed circuit of sympathy with Piggy outside: he went very pink, bowed his head and cleaned his glasses again.

36 Finally the laughter died away and the naming continued. There was Maurice, next in size among the choir boys to Jack, but broad and grinning all the time. There was a slight, furtiveboy whom no one knew, who kept to himself with an inner intensity of avoidance and secrecy. He muttered that his name was Roger and was silent again. Bill, Robert, Harold, Henry; the choir boy who had fainted sat up against a palm trunk, smiled **pallidly** at Ralph and said that his name was Simon.

37 Jack spoke.

38 "We've got to decide about being rescued."

39 There was a buzz. One of the small boys, Henry, said that he wanted to go home.

40 "Shut up," said Ralph absently. He lifted the conch. "Seems to me we ought to have a chief to decide things."

41 "A chief! A chief!"

42 "I ought to be chief," said Jack with simple arrogance, "because I'm chapter chorister and head boy. I can sing C sharp."

43 Another buzz.

44 "Well then," said Jack, "I—"

45 He hesitated. The dark boy, Roger, stirred at last and spoke up.

46 "Let's have a vote."

47 "Yes!"

48 "Vote for chief!"

49 "Let's vote—"

50 This toy of voting was almost as pleasing as the conch. Jack started to protest but the clamor changed from the general wish for a chief to an election by acclaim of Ralph himself. None of the boys could have found good reason for this; what intelligence had been shown was traceable to Piggy while the most

obvious leader was Jack. But there was a stillness about Ralph as he sat that marked him out: there was his size, and attractive appearance; and most obscurely, yet most powerfully, there was the conch. The being that had blown that, had sat waiting for them on the platform with the delicate thing balanced on his knees, was set apart.

51 "Him with the shell."

52 "Ralph! Ralph!"

53 "Let him be chief with the trumpet-thing."

54 Ralph raised a hand for silence.

55 "All right. Who wants Jack for chief?"

56 With dreary obedience the choir raised their hands.

57 "Who wants me?"

58 Every hand outside the choir except Piggy's was raised immediately. Then Piggy, too, raised his hand grudgingly into the air.

59 Ralph counted.

60 "I'm chief then."

61 The circle of boys broke into applause. Even the choir applauded; and the freckles on Jack's face disappeared under a blush of **mortification.** He started up, then changed his mind and sat down again while the air rang. Ralph looked at him, eager to offer something.

62 "The choir belongs to you, of course."

63 "They could be the army—"

64 "Or hunters—"

65 "They could be—"

66 The **suffusion** drained away from Jack's face.

. . .

67 The three boys walked briskly on the sand. The tide was low and there was a strip of weed-strewn beach that was almost as firm as a road. A kind of glamour was spread over them and the scene and they were conscious of

the glamour and made happy by it. They turned to each other, laughing excitedly, talking, not listening. The air was bright. Ralph, faced by the task of translating all this into an explanation, stood on his head and fell over. When they had done laughing, Simon stroked Ralph's arm shyly; and they had to laugh again.

68. "Come on," said Jack presently, "we're explorers."

Excerpted from *Lord of the Flies* by William Golding, published by The Berkley Publishing Group.

THINK QUESTIONS

1. What has happened that has caused the boys to be where they are? Explain your inferences about where they are and what happened using textual evidence.

2. Why must the boys choose a leader, and what role does the conch shell play? Explain your answer using evidence from the text.

3. What can you infer about the characters of Ralph and Jack? Use textual evidence to explain your inferences.

4. The Latin root of the word **furtive** is *fur,* meaning "thief." Using this knowledge and context clues, determine the meaning of the word "furtive" as it is used in paragraph 36 of *Lord of the Flies*. Write your definition of furtive and tell how you figured it out.

5. Remembering that the Latin root *mort* means "death," use your knowledge of the Latin root and the context clues provided in the passage to determine the meaning of **mortification**. Write your definition of "mortification" and tell how you figured it out.

STUDYSYNC LIBRARY | Lord of the Flies

CLOSE READ

Reread the excerpt from *Lord of the Flies*. As you reread, complete the Focus Questions below. Then use your answers and annotations from the questions to help you complete the Writing Prompt.

FOCUS QUESTIONS

1. As you reread the excerpt from *The Lord of the Flies*, focus on the character of Jack Merridew. What do his words and actions reveal about his character? Why do you think he wants to be called Merridew instead of Jack? Ask and answer your own question about Jack's character.

2. Analyze the character of Piggy in the novel excerpt. How do his words and actions, as well as the narrator's descriptions, reveal aspects of his character? How do the other boys treat Piggy, and how and why does this treatment reflect negatively on human nature?

3. In this excerpt, the boys choose a leader. Why do they choose Ralph? Is it because they think he will be the best leader or for some other reason? What possible theme might Golding be exploring through the election and its results?

4. What might the mysterious conch symbolize? Why might it hold such a strange power over the boys? What possible theme in the novel might Golding be exploring through the conch?

5. In *The Lord of the Flies*, Golding explores the theme of civilization. Based on evidence throughout the excerpt, what tension exists between the boys' ideas about civilization and their behavior toward one another?

6. The story is a classic in literature as well as being very popular. Summarize the events that take place in this excerpt from the story. What do you think has attracted readers to the story's conflicts and suspense? Use text evidence to describe how the reader is drawn into the story's plot.

WRITING PROMPT

Think about the relationship between the characters of Ralph and Piggy as revealed in this excerpt. How does Jack Merridew affect this relationship? Use your understanding of character and theme to examine the relationship between Ralph and Piggy and what it might suggest about the rules and challenges of friendship.

TEN DAYS IN A MADHOUSE
(CHAPTER IV)

NON-FICTION
Nellie Bly
1887

INTRODUCTION

In 1887, reporter Nellie Bly went on an undercover assignment for a New York newspaper, the *World*, for which she feigned insanity in order to get committed to the Blackwell's Island Insane Asylum. Her exposé of the conditions inside the Women's Lunatic Asylum launched a criminal investigation that later led to an $850,000 budget increase from the Department of Public Charities and Corrections. *Ten Days in a Mad-House* began as a series of newspaper articles and was eventually published as a book.

"At last the question of my sanity or insanity was to be decided."

FIRST READ

Chapter IV: Judge Duffy and the Police

1 "Are you Nellie Brown?" asked the officer. I said I supposed I was. "Where do you come from?" he asked. I told him I did not know, and then Mrs. Stanard gave him a lot of information about me—told him how strangely I had acted at her home; how I had not slept a wink all night, and that in her opinion I was a poor unfortunate who had been driven crazy by inhuman treatment. There was some discussion between Mrs. Standard and the two officers, and Tom Bockert was told to take us down to the court in a car.

2 "Come along," Bockert said, "I will find your trunk for you." We all went together, Mrs. Stanard, Tom Bockert, and myself. I said it was very kind of them to go with me, and I should not soon forget them. As we walked along I kept up my refrain about my trunks, injecting occasionally some remark about the dirty condition of the streets and the curious character of the people we met on the way. "I don't think I have ever seen such people before," I said. "Who are they?" I asked, and my companions looked upon me with expressions of pity, evidently believing I was a foreigner, an emigrant or something of the sort. They told me that the people around me were working people. I remarked once more that I thought there were too many working people in the world for the amount of work to be done, at which remark Policeman P. T. Bockert eyed me closely, evidently thinking that my mind was gone for good. We passed several other policemen, who generally asked my sturdy guardians what was the matter with me. By this time quite a number of ragged children were following us too, and they passed remarks about me that were to me original as well as amusing.

3 "What's she up for?" "Say, kop, where did ye get her?" "Where did yer pull 'er?" "She's a daisy!"

4. Poor Mrs. Stanard was more frightened than I was. The whole situation grew interesting, but I still had fears for my fate before the judge.

5. At last we came to a low building, and Tom Bockert kindly volunteered the information: "Here's the express office. We shall soon find those trunks of yours."

6. The entrance to the building was surrounded by a curious crowd and I did not think my case was bad enough to permit me passing them without some remark, so I asked if all those people had lost their trunks.

7. "Yes," he said, "nearly all these people are looking for trunks."

8. I said, "They all seem to be foreigners, too." "Yes," said Tom, "they are all foreigners just landed. They have all lost their trunks, and it takes most of our time to help find them for them."

9. We entered the courtroom. It was the Essex Market Police Courtroom. At last the question of my sanity or insanity was to be decided. Judge Duffy sat behind the high desk, wearing a look which seemed to indicate that he was dealing out the **milk of human kindness** by wholesale. I rather feared I would not get the fate I sought, because of the kindness I saw on every line of his face, and it was with rather a sinking heart that I followed Mrs. Stanard as she answered the summons to go up to the desk, where Tom Bockert had just given an account of the affair.

10. "Come here," said an officer. "What is your name?"

11. "Nellie Brown," I replied, with a little accent. "I have lost my trunks, and would like if you could find them."

12. "When did you come to New York?" he asked.

13. "I did not come to New York," I replied (while I added, mentally, "because I have been here for some time.")

14. "But you are in New York now," said the man.

15. "No," I said, looking as **incredulous** as I thought a crazy person could, "I did not come to New York."

16. "That girl is from the west," he said, in a tone that made me tremble. "She has a western accent."

17. Someone else who had been listening to the brief dialogue here asserted that he had lived south and that my accent was southern, while another officer

was positive it was eastern. I felt much relieved when the first spokesman turned to the judge and said:

18 "Judge, here is a peculiar case of a young woman who doesn't know who she is or where she came from. You had better attend to it at once."

19 I commenced to shake with more than the cold, and I looked around at the strange crowd about me, composed of poorly dressed men and women with stories printed on their faces of hard lives, abuse and poverty. Some were consulting eagerly with friends, while others sat still with a look of utter hopelessness. Everywhere was a sprinkling of well-dressed, well-fed officers watching the scene passively and almost indifferently. It was only an old story with them. One more unfortunate added to a long list which had long since ceased to be of any interest or concern to them.

20 "Come here, girl, and lift your veil," called out Judge Duffy, in tones which surprised me by a harshness which I did not think from the kindly face he possessed.

21 "Who are you speaking to?" I inquired, in my stateliest manner.

22 "Come here, my dear, and lift your veil. You know the Queen of England, if she were here, would have to lift her veil," he said, very kindly.

23 "That is much better," I replied. "I am not the Queen of England, but I'll lift my veil."

24 As I did so the little judge looked at me, and then, in a very kind and gentle tone, he said: "My dear child, what is wrong?"

25 "Nothing is wrong except that I have lost my trunks, and this man," indicating Policeman Bockert, "promised to bring me where they could be found."

26 "What do you know about this child?" asked the judge, sternly, of Mrs. Stanard, who stood, pale and trembling, by my side.

27 "I know nothing of her except that she came to the home yesterday and asked to remain overnight."

28 "The home! What do you mean by the home?" asked Judge Duffy, quickly.

29 "It is a temporary home kept for working women at No. 84 Second Avenue."

30 "What is your position there?"

31 "I am assistant **matron**."

32 "Well, tell us all you know of the case."

33 "When I was going into the home yesterday I noticed her coming down the avenue. She was all alone. I had just got into the house when the bell rang and she came in. When I talked with her she wanted to know if she could stay all night, and I said she could. After awhile she said all the people in the house looked crazy, and she was afraid of them. Then she would not go to bed, but sat up all the night."

34 "Had she any money?"

35 "Yes," I replied, answering for her, "I paid her for everything, and the eating was the worst I ever tried."

36 There was a general smile at this, and some murmurs of "She's not so crazy on the food question."

37 "Poor child," said Judge Duffy, "she is well dressed, and a lady. Her English is perfect, and I would stake everything on her being a good girl. I am positive she is somebody's darling."

38 At this announcement everybody laughed, and I put my handkerchief over my face and endeavored to choke the laughter that threatened to spoil my plans, in despite of my resolutions.

39 "I mean she is some woman's darling," hastily amended the judge. "I am sure someone is searching for her. Poor girl, I will be good to her, for she looks like my sister, who is dead."

40 There was a hush for a moment after this announcement, and the officers glanced at me more kindly, while I silently blessed the kind-hearted judge, and hoped that any poor creatures who might be afflicted as I pretended to be should have as kindly a man to deal with as Judge Duffy.

41 "I wish the reporters were here," he said at last. "They would be able to find out something about her."

42 I got very much frightened at this, for if there is anyone who can **ferret out** a mystery it is a reporter. I felt that I would rather face a mass of expert doctors, policemen, and detectives than two bright specimens of my craft, so I said:

43 "I don't see why all this is needed to help me find my trunks. These men are **impudent,** and I do not want to be stared at. I will go away. I don't want to stay here."

44. So saying, I pulled down my veil and secretly hoped the reporters would be detained elsewhere until I was sent to the asylum.

45. "I don't know what to do with the poor child," said the worried judge. "She must be taken care of."

46. "Send her to the Island," suggested one of the officers.

47. "Oh, don't!" said Mrs. Stanard, in evident alarm. "Don't! She is a lady and it would kill her to be put on the Island."

48. For once I felt like shaking the good woman. To think the Island was just the place I wanted to reach and here she was trying to keep me from going there! It was very kind of her, but rather provoking under the circumstances.

THINK QUESTIONS

1. What can you infer about what Nellie Bly is like as a reporter and a person? Write a response in which you describe Nellie based on what you learn about her from the passage. Cite evidence from the text to support your inferences.

2. What is the main point Nellie Bly makes in this chapter as she tries to get into the asylum? Cite textual evidence to support your ideas.

3. When Nellie Bly describes the people around her as having "stories printed on their faces of hard lives, abuse and poverty," and that it is "only an old story" to the court, what does she mean? Cite evidence from the text to support your response.

4. Use context to determine the meaning of the word **impudent** as it is used in *Ten Days in a Mad-House*. Write your definition of "impudent" and tell how you figured it out.

5. Remembering that the Latin prefix *in-* means "not," and the Latin root *cred* means "believe or trust," use this knowledge to determine the meaning of **incredulous**. Write your definition of "incredulous" and tell how you figured it out. Use a print or digital dictionary to verify your meaning.

CLOSE READ

Reread the excerpt from *Ten Days in a Mad-House*. As you reread, complete the Focus Questions below. Then use your answers and annotations from the questions to help you complete the Writing Prompt.

FOCUS QUESTIONS

1. Reread the first eight paragraphs of *Ten Days in a Mad-House*. Based on details in Nellie Bly's description of her journey to the courthouse, what is her point of view about how society perceives and treats those taken into custody by the police?

2. In paragraph 19, the author describes the officers in the courtroom. What words does she use to describe them? What do these words reveal about her point of view toward the court officials?

3. In paragraph 40, the author says that she "silently blessed the kind-hearted judge." Why does she do so? What does this tell you about her point of view about the way that the poor, particularly those who are mentally ill, are treated in the legal system?

4. Based on details throughout the passage, how would you describe Nellie's Bly's overall reporting style? How might this style have encouraged readers to share her point of view and have contributed to the impact *Ten Days in a Mad-House* had on changing New York City's treatment of the mentally ill?

5. The excerpt contains dramatic irony. Dramatic irony occurs when the reader or audience knows something that the characters or subjects do not know. Dramatic irony can be used to create effects such as humor or suspense. Write a response in which you explain the use of dramatic irony in the passage. Use your understanding of point of view to explain how the author uses dramatic irony to reveal her point of view and to develop suspense that keeps the reader interested.

WRITING PROMPT

What is Nellie Bly's point of view about the plight of the poor and mentally ill and the attitudes of officials toward these people? How does she use humor, dramatic irony, and descriptive adjectives to reveal her opinions? What do Bly's opinions and actions tell you about her as a person? Support your writing with evidence from the text.

THE TELL-TALE HEART

FICTION
Edgar Allen Poe
1843

INTRODUCTION

studysync

Edgar Allan Poe's short story "The Tell-Tale Heart" sets the standard for Gothic fiction. Convinced that officers at his house can hear the dead man's heart beating through the floorboard, Poe's narrator confesses to killing an old man in his care, despite the fact he bore the man no grudge. In a dramatic monologue of increasing volume and intensity—as well as mental disintegration-- the "perfectly sane" murderer painstakingly describes how the "vulture eye" of his victim drove him to commit the horrible act.

"His eye would trouble me no more."

FIRST READ

1. TRUE! nervous, very, very dreadfully nervous I had been and am; but why WILL you say that I am mad? The disease had sharpened my senses, not destroyed, not dulled them. Above all was the sense of hearing acute. I heard all things in the heaven and in the earth. I heard many things in hell. How then am I mad? Hearken! and observe how healthily, how calmly, I can tell you the whole story.

2. It is impossible to say how first the idea entered my brain, but, once conceived, it haunted me day and night. Object there was none. Passion there was none. I loved the old man. He had never wronged me. He had never given me insult. For his gold I had no desire. I think it was his eye! Yes, it was this! One of his eyes resembled that of a vulture -- a pale blue eye with a film over it. Whenever it fell upon me my blood ran cold, and so by degrees, very gradually, I made up my mind to take the life of the old man, and thus rid myself of the eye forever.

3. Now this is the point. You fancy me mad. Madmen know nothing. But you should have seen me. You should have seen how wisely I proceeded—with what caution—with what foresight, with what **dissimulation,** I went to work! I was never kinder to the old man than during the whole week before I killed him. And every night about midnight I turned the latch of his door and opened it oh, so gently! And then, when I had made an opening sufficient for my head, I put in a dark lantern all closed, closed so that no light shone out, and then I thrust in my head. Oh, you would have laughed to see how cunningly I thrust it in! I moved it slowly, very, very slowly, so that I might not disturb the old man's sleep. It took me an hour to place my whole head within the opening so far that I could see him as he lay upon his bed. Ha! would a madman have been so wise as this? And then when my head was well in the room I undid the lantern cautiously— oh, so cautiously—cautiously (for the hinges creaked), I undid it just so much that a single thin ray fell upon the vulture eye. And this I did for seven long nights, every night just at midnight, but I found the eye

always closed, and so it was impossible to do the work, for it was not the old man who **vexed** me but his Evil Eye. And every morning, when the day broke, I went boldly into the chamber and spoke courageously to him, calling him by name in a hearty tone, and inquiring how he had passed the night. So you see he would have been a very profound old man, indeed, to suspect that every night, just at twelve, I looked in upon him while he slept.

4   Upon the eighth night I was more than usually cautious in opening the door. A watch's minute hand moves more quickly than did mine. Never before that night had I felt the extent of my own powers, of my **sagacity.** I could scarcely contain my feelings of triumph. To think that there I was opening the door little by little, and he not even to dream of my secret deeds or thoughts. I fairly chuckled at the idea, and perhaps he heard me, for he moved on the bed suddenly as if startled. Now you may think that I drew back—but no. His room was as black as pitch with the thick darkness (for the shutters were close fastened through fear of robbers), and so I knew that he could not see the opening of the door, and I kept pushing it on steadily, steadily.

5   I had my head in, and was about to open the lantern, when my thumb slipped upon the tin fastening, and the old man sprang up in the bed, crying out, "Who's there?"

6   I kept quite still and said nothing. For a whole hour I did not move a muscle, and in the meantime I did not hear him lie down. He was still sitting up in the bed, listening; just as I have done night after night hearkening to the death watches in the wall.

7   Presently, I heard a slight groan, and I knew it was the groan of mortal terror. It was not a groan of pain or of grief—oh, no! It was the low stifled sound that arises from the bottom of the soul when overcharged with awe. I knew the sound well. Many a night, just at midnight, when all the world slept, it has welled up from my own bosom, deepening, with its dreadful echo, the terrors that distracted me. I say I knew it well. I knew what the old man felt, and pitied him although I chuckled at heart. I knew that he had been lying awake ever since the first slight noise when he had turned in the bed. His fears had been ever since growing upon him. He had been trying to fancy them causeless, but could not. He had been saying to himself, "It is nothing but the wind in the chimney, it is only a mouse crossing the floor," or, "It is merely a cricket which has made a single chirp." Yes he has been trying to comfort himself with these suppositions; but he had found all in vain. ALL IN VAIN, because Death in approaching him had stalked with his black shadow before him and enveloped the victim. And it was the mournful influence of the unperceived shadow that caused him to feel, although he neither saw nor heard, to feel the presence of my head within the room.

8. When I had waited a long time very patiently without hearing him lie down, I resolved to open a little—a very, very little crevice in the lantern. So I opened it—you cannot imagine how stealthily, stealthily—until at length a single dim ray like the thread of the spider shot out from the crevice and fell upon the vulture eye.

9. It was open, wide, wide open, and I grew furious as I gazed upon it. I saw it with perfect distinctness—all a dull blue with a hideous veil over it that chilled the very marrow in my bones, but I could see nothing else of the old man's face or person, for I had directed the ray as if by instinct precisely upon the damned spot.

10. And now have I not told you that what you mistake for madness is but over-acuteness of the senses? now, I say, there came to my ears a low, dull, quick sound, such as a watch makes when enveloped in cotton. I knew that sound well too. It was the beating of the old man's heart. It increased my fury as the beating of a drum stimulates the soldier into courage.

11. But even yet I refrained and kept still. I scarcely breathed. I held the lantern motionless. I tried how steadily I could maintain the ray upon the eye. Meantime the hellish tattoo of the heart increased. It grew quicker and quicker, and louder and louder, every instant. The old man's terror must have been extreme! It grew louder, I say, louder every moment! —do you mark me well? I have told you that I am nervous: so I am. And now at the dead hour of the night, amid the dreadful silence of that old house, so strange a noise as this excited me to uncontrollable terror. Yet, for some minutes longer I refrained and stood still. But the beating grew louder, louder! I thought the heart must burst. And now a new anxiety seized me—the sound would be heard by a neighbour! The old man's hour had come! With a loud yell, I threw open the lantern and leaped into the room. He shrieked once—once only. In an instant I dragged him to the floor, and pulled the heavy bed over him. I then smiled gaily, to find the deed so far done. But for many minutes the heart beat on with a muffled sound. This, however, did not vex me; it would not be heard through the wall. At length it ceased. The old man was dead. I removed the bed and examined the corpse. Yes, he was stone, stone dead. I placed my hand upon the heart and held it there many minutes. There was no pulsation. He was stone dead. His eye would trouble me no more.

12. If still you think me mad, you will think so no longer when I describe the wise precautions I took for the concealment of the body. The night waned, and I worked hastily, but in silence.

13. I took up three planks from the flooring of the chamber, and deposited all between the scantlings. I then replaced the boards so cleverly so cunningly, that no human eye—not even his—could have detected anything wrong.

I had been too wary for that. There was nothing to wash out—no stain of any kind—no blood-spot whatever.

14 When I had made an end of these labours, it was four o'clock—still dark as midnight. As the bell sounded the hour, there came a knocking at the street door. I went down to open it with a light heart, —for what had I now to fear? There entered three men, who introduced themselves, with perfect suavity, as officers of the police. A shriek had been heard by a neighbour during the night; suspicion of foul play had been aroused; information had been lodged at the police office, and they (the officers) had been deputed to search the premises.

15 I smiled, —for what had I to fear? I bade the gentlemen welcome. The shriek, I said, was my own in a dream. The old man, I mentioned, was absent in the country. I took my visitors all over the house. I bade them search—search well. I led them, at length, to his chamber. I showed them his treasures, secure, undisturbed. In the enthusiasm of my confidence, I brought chairs into the room, and desired them here to rest from their fatigues, while I myself, in the wild audacity of my perfect triumph, placed my own seat upon the very spot beneath which reposed the corpse of the victim.

16 The officers were satisfied. My MANNER had convinced them. I was singularly at ease. They sat and while I answered cheerily, they chatted of familiar things. But, ere long, I felt myself getting pale and wished them gone. My head ached, and I fancied a ringing in my ears; but still they sat, and still chatted. The ringing became more distinct: I talked more freely to get rid of the feeling: but it continued and gained definitiveness—until, at length, I found that the noise was NOT within my ears.

17 No doubt I now grew VERY pale; but I talked more fluently, and with a heightened voice. Yet the sound increased -- and what could I do? It was A LOW, DULL, QUICK SOUND -- MUCH SUCH A SOUND AS A WATCH MAKES WHEN ENVELOPED IN COTTON. I gasped for breath, and yet the officers heard it not. I talked more quickly, more vehemently but the noise steadily increased. I arose and argued about trifles, in a high key and with violent gesticulations; but the noise steadily increased. Why WOULD they not be gone? I paced the floor to and fro with heavy strides, as if excited to fury by the observations of the men, but the noise steadily increased. O God! what COULD I do? I foamed—I raved—I swore! I swung the chair upon which I had been sitting, and grated it upon the boards, but the noise arose over all and continually increased. It grew louder—louder—louder! And still the men chatted pleasantly, and smiled. Was it possible they heard not? Almighty God! —no, no? They heard! —they suspected! —they KNEW! —they were making a mockery of my horror! —this I thought, and this I think. But anything was better than this agony! Anything was more tolerable than this derision! I could bear

those hypocritical smiles no longer! I felt that I must scream or die! —and now —again —hark! louder! louder! louder! LOUDER! —

18 "Villains!" I shrieked, **"dissemble** no more! I admit the deed! —tear up the planks! —here, here! —it is the beating of his hideous heart!"

THINK QUESTIONS

1. Citing evidence from the story, briefly explain how the narrator feels about the old man and why he decides to murder him. What can you infer about the narrator? Explain your inference.

2. Is the first-person narrator trustworthy as he gives his account of the events in the story? Cite textual evidence to explain your opinions.

3. What sound does the narrator hear at the end of the story that causes him to confess to the murder? What effect does the narration have on the story? Provide textual evidence to support your inference.

4. Use context to determine the meaning of the word **vexed** as it is used in *The Tell-Tale Heart*. Write your definition of "vexed" and explain how you figured it out.

5. Remembering that the Latin prefix *dis-* means "not," use your knowledge of the prefix and the context clues in the passage to determine the meaning of **dissemble.** Write your definition of "dissemble" and explain how you arrived at it.

STUDYSYNC LIBRARY | The Tell-Tale Heart

CLOSE READ

Reread the short story "The Tell-Tale Heart." As you reread, complete the Focus Questions below. Then use your answers and annotations from the questions to help you complete the Writing Prompt.

FOCUS QUESTIONS

1. What central ideas about the narrator of "The Tell-Tale Heart" does Edgar Allan Poe intend readers to infer, based on textual evidence throughout the story? Based on what he does, what he says, and what he doesn't say, describe the narrator's state of mind in the aftermath of committing murder and what this suggests about his character. Use the strategies you learned about making inferences. First, find facts, details, and examples that can help make a reasonable guess. Second, use your own knowledge, experiences, and observations to figure out things the author doesn't directly state. Third, read closely and critically, thinking about why the author provides certain details and information but not others. Cite textual evidence and write annotations to explain your understanding.

2. What motivation for his actions does the narrator offer in paragraph 2? How does the narrator likely intend his audience to react to his motivation for murder? What actual reaction will readers likely have, based on the details he provides? Use textual evidence to explore the contrast between what the narrator intends to demonstrate about his character and what he ends up revealing in this paragraph.

3. Poe's narrator twice uses the word *corpse*, in paragraphs 11 and 15. *Corpse* comes from the Latin root *corpus*, meaning "body." Using your knowledge of this Latin root, as well as context clues and any prior knowledge, define the word *corpse*. Why do you think the narrator uses this specific word in his narrative of events? Cite textual evidence to explain your ideas.

4. The particular character of the narrator in this story may affect what details are presented directly, as well as those the readers are intended to infer. Based on the details in the first paragraph, how is the narrator relating these events? In paragraphs 3 and 4, how does this narration affect readers' impression of the narrator and interpretation of the events that have taken place?

5. Authors of Gothic tales such as "The Tell-Tale Heart" often use symbols to help develop the theme of a story. The "vulture eye" and "the beating heart" are examples of two key symbols used in this way. Highlight several instances of the author's use of these symbols. Make annotations to interpret the significance of these symbols and describe how they contribute to the story's theme.

6. There's no denying that "The Tell-Tale Heart" is a gruesome story. A mentally and emotionally unstable narrator gets an insane idea in his head and savagely murders an innocent old man who trusts him. Yet the story is among Poe's most popular works, and is read with pleasure by every succeeding generation. Why do people enjoy suspense and horror stories like this one? Is it despite—or because of—their dreadful details? Use evidence from the story to support your answer.

WRITING PROMPT

Suppose you are the narrator's attorney, assigned to defend him in the aftermath of the murder he committed. Since the narrator freely admitted to the police that he committed the crime, you have decided to have him enter a plea of "not guilty by reason of insanity." First, identify evidence in the text that you believe most strongly illustrates the narrator's psychological state before, during, and after the murder. Then, identify details that you would advise the narrator to leave out during his testimony, as they reflect poorly on his character and might alienate or offend the jury. Finally, based on text evidence, construct a brief "closing argument" to the jury that makes the case that the narrator is not guilty by reason of insanity for the crime of murder.

ANNABEL LEE

POETRY
Edgar Allen Poe
1849

INTRODUCTION

Edgar Allan Poe's last complete poem, "Annabel Lee," follows a familiar Poe storyline—the death of a beautiful woman. Poe lost many women close to him over the course of his life, and there has been much speculation and debate about who served as the inspiration for "Annabel Lee". Most people believe that Poe wrote the poem about his late wife, Virginia Clemm, who died of tuberculosis in 1847.

"But we loved with a love that was more than love—"

FIRST READ

1 It was many and many a year ago,
2   In a kingdom by the sea
3 That a maiden there lived whom you may know
4   By the name of Annabel Lee;
5 And this maiden she lived with no other thought
6   Than to love and be loved by me.

7 She was a child and I was a child,
8   In this kingdom by the sea,
9 But we loved with a love that was more than love—
10   I and my Annabel Lee—
11 With a love that the wingèd **seraphs** of heaven
12   **Coveted** her and me.

13 And this was the reason that, long ago,
14   In this kingdom by the sea,
15 A wind blew out of a cloud by night
16   Chilling my Annabel Lee;
17 So that her high-born **kinsmen** came
18   And bore her away from me,
19 To shut her up in a **sepulchre**
20   In this kingdom by the sea.

21 The angels, not half so happy in heaven,
22   Went envying her and me—
23 Yes!—that was the reason (as all men know,
24   In this kingdom by the sea)
25 That the wind came out of the cloud, chilling
26   And killing my Annabel Lee.

STUDYSYNC LIBRARY | Annabel Lee

27 But our love it was stronger by far than the love
28   Of those who were older than we—
29   Of many far wiser than we—
30 And neither the angels in heaven above,
31   Nor the demons down under the sea,
32 Can ever **dissever** my soul from the soul
33   Of the beautiful Annabel Lee:

34 For the moon never beams, without bringing me dreams
35   Of the beautiful Annabel Lee,
36 And the stars never rise, but I see the bright eyes
37   Of the beautiful Annabel Lee:
38 And so, all the night-tide, I lie down by the side
39   Of my darling—my darling—my life and my bride,
40   In the sepulchre there by the sea—
41   In her tomb by the side of the sea.

THINK QUESTIONS

1. What is the relationship between the speaker of the poem and Annabel Lee? What happens during the course of the poem to change that relationship? Use ideas that are directly stated and ideas that you have inferred from clues in the text to explain your answer.

2. Using what the text explicitly says, as well as what you have inferred, is the speaker reliable? Do you believe everything he says? Is there anything in the poem that would give you reason to doubt what he says?

3. Think about the words, sounds, and rhythms that Poe uses throughout the poem. What kinds of images do the words create? What sort of feeling does the author create at the beginning, and does it change? Cite textual examples to explain your ideas.

4. Use context to determine the meaning of the word **seraphs** as it is used in line 11 of "Annabel Lee." Write your definition of "seraphs" and explain how you figured it out.

5. Find the word **dissever** in the poem. Identify the context clues that support its meaning. Write the definition of "dissever" based on the context clues and explain how you figured it out. Then use a dictionary to verify the meaning. Was your meaning correct?

STUDYSYNC LIBRARY | Annabel Lee

CLOSE READ

Reread the poem "Annabel Lee." As you reread, complete the Focus Questions below. Then use your answers and annotations from the questions to help you complete the Writing Prompt.

FOCUS QUESTIONS

1. As you reread the poem "Annabel Lee," highlight examples of interesting rhyming words within the lines and at the ends of lines. In addition, highlight examples of words and phrases that are repeated. In an annotation, explain the effect of these rhymes and repetitions, expressed in a repetitive rhythm, on the subject of the poem. What tone or feeling does Poe create through his word choice?

2. The speaker of the poem believes that the loss of his love, Annabel Lee, is an event worth sharing with the world. In what figurative terms does the speaker frame his love and his loss, and how is this intended to heighten readers' sense of their importance? Highlight relevant words, phrases, and lines in the first two stanzas. Annotate to explain how the speaker's feelings about his love and loss are revealed in this section of the poem.

3. Highlight the various words the speaker uses to refer to Annabel Lee. How much does the reader learn about who Annabel Lee was a person? How does the speaker see Annabel Lee? Explain what the speaker's characterization of Annabel Lee reveals about his own character.

4. Highlight words and phrases that strike you as unusual or unsettling in the poem. What makes this poem different from a simple love poem? Explain how this love poem contains elements of a horror story.

5. How does Poe build suspense in the poem as the stanzas progress from beginning to end? In what way does this suspense continue even after the "climax," or turning point in the story the poem tells, compelling readers to keep going—even if they fear what lies ahead?

WRITING PROMPT

Identify those lines in the poem that most clearly allow you to follow the "story" of the poem. Then retell the story of the poem in prose. Finally, explain what the poem loses when it becomes a prose story rather than a poem. How does the poem's rhythm and rhyme, as well as other poetic elements, support its theme or message? Use evidence from the text, as well as from comparing your retelling with that of the poem itself, to support your response.

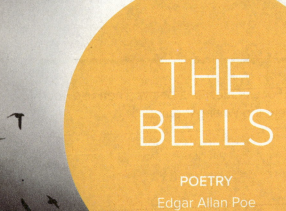

THE BELLS

POETRY
Edgar Allan Poe
1849

INTRODUCTION

Not published until shortly after his death in 1849, Edgar Allan Poe is said to have been inspired to write "The Bells" by a comment from the woman who cared for his dying wife, Virginia. Living near enough to hear Fordham University's bell tower, Poe asked the nurse for a poem topic, and Mrs. Shew suggested the ringing bells for a starting point. The heavily onomatopoeic poem has been interpreted in different ways.

"Keeping time, time, time..."

FIRST READ

I

1 Hear the sledges with the bells—
2 Silver bells!
3 What a world of merriment their melody foretells!
4 How they tinkle, tinkle, tinkle,
5 In the icy air of night!
6 While the stars that oversprinkle
7 All the heavens, seem to twinkle
8 With a crystalline delight;
9 Keeping time, time, time,
10 In a sort of **Runic** rhyme,
11 To the **tintinnabulation** that so musically wells
12 From the bells, bells, bells, bells,
13 Bells, bells, bells—
14 From the jingling and the tinkling of the bells.

II

15 Hear the mellow wedding bells—
16 Golden bells!
17 What a world of happiness their harmony foretells!
18 Through the balmy air of night
19 How they ring out their delight!—
20 From the **molten**-golden notes,
21 And all in tune,
22 What a liquid **ditty** floats
23 To the turtle-dove that listens, while she gloats
24 On the moon!
25 Oh, from out the sounding cells,
26 What a gush of **euphony voluminously** wells!

STUDYSYNC LIBRARY | The Bells

27 How it swells!
28 How it dwells
29 On the Future!—how it tells
30 Of the rapture that impels
31 To the swinging and the ringing
32 Of the bells, bells, bells—
33 Of the bells, bells, bells, bells,
34 Bells, bells, bells—
35 To the rhyming and the chiming of the bells!

III

36 Hear the loud **alarum** bells—
37 Brazen bells!
38 What a tale of terror, now, their turbulency tells!
39 In the startled ear of night
40 How they scream out their affright!
41 Too much horrified to speak,
42 They can only shriek, shriek,
43 Out of tune,
44 In a clamorous appealing to the mercy of the fire,
45 In a mad expostulation with the deaf and frantic fire,
46 Leaping higher, higher, higher,
47 With a desperate desire,
48 And a resolute endeavor
49 Now—now to sit, or never,
50 By the side of the pale-faced moon.
51 Oh, the bells, bells, bells!
52 What a tale their terror tells
53 Of Despair!
54 How they clang, and clash and roar!
55 What a horror they outpour
56 On the bosom of the palpitating air!
57 Yet the ear, it fully knows,
58 By the twanging,
59 And the clanging,
60 How the danger ebbs and flows;
61 Yet the ear distinctly tells,
62 In the jangling,
63 And the wrangling,
64 How the danger sinks and swells,
65 By the sinking or the swelling in the anger of the bells—
66 Of the bells—
67 Of the bells, bells, bells, bells,

CLOSE READ

Reread the poem "The Bells." As you reread, complete the Focus Questions below. Then use your answers and annotations from the questions to help you complete the Writing Prompt.

FOCUS QUESTIONS

1. *Onomatopoeia* is the use of words to represent specific sounds. As you reread "The Bells," highlight examples of onomatopoeia that you see in the first and third stanzas. How do the examples of onomatopoeia change from stanza to stanza? How do the sounds of the words create a feeling or mood? Write annotations to explain your ideas.

2. In his poem, Poe includes a great deal of alliteration, which is the repetition of consonant sounds at the beginnings of words—such as the *w* and the *m* in "What a world of merriment their melody foretells" in the first stanza. Highlight a few examples of alliteration in the third stanza of the poem. Annotate to describe the effect the consonant sounds create.

3. Poe has arranged the poem in four stanzas. What is the theme or central idea in each stanza? Write an annotation by each stanza, highlighting textual evidence to support your ideas. Finally, what do you think the poem is about? Summarize the poem's ideas in another annotation.

4. Highlight the line that includes the word *euphony* in the second stanza. Reread the definition of *euphony* and annotate to explain why the author would think this is a good word to use in this poem. How does the idea of euphony contrast with the way the bells change in the poem? Highlight text that seems to contrast to euphony. Annotate to explain your understanding.

5. Personification is representing an inanimate thing or an idea as a person. Highlight examples of personification in the third and fourth stanzas and annotate to explore how these examples affect the poem's meaning and tone.

6. How does Poe use word choice, sound devices, imagery, and other poetic elements to give the poem a feeling of terror and suspense? Use evidence from the text to support your answer.

WRITING PROMPT

An alternate reading of "The Bells" is that the poem's theme is about the changing of the seasons, as opposed to the story of a tragic loss and subsequent grief. Choose one theme and use text evidence, including examples of specific word choices, as well as personal experience and inference, to defend your interpretation of the poem's theme.

NARRATIVE WRITING

WRITING PROMPT

You have been reading and learning about stories of suspense, in addition to studying techniques authors use to generate a feeling of suspense in readers. Now you will use those techniques to write your own suspenseful narrative based on real or imagined experiences and events.

Your essay should include:
- a plot with a beginning, middle, and end
- a clear setting
- characters and dialogue
- a suspenseful theme

Narrative writing tells a story of real or imagined experiences or events. Narratives can be fiction, such as stories and poems, or non-fiction, such as memoirs and personal essays. Good narrative writing uses effective techniques, relevant descriptive details, and well-structured event sequences to convey a story to readers.

The features of narrative writing include:
- setting
- characters
- plot
- theme
- point of view

As you continue with this extended writing project, you'll receive more instruction and practice crafting each of the elements of narrative writing to create your own suspenseful narrative.

STUDYSYNC LIBRARY | Extended Writing Project

STUDENT MODEL

Before you get started on your own suspenseful narrative, read this excerpt from the beginning of a narrative that one student wrote in response to the writing prompt. As you read the model, highlight and annotate the features of narrative writing that this student included in her story.

The Silver Box

The night was so clear that if the Carey family had been standing in the front yard, beneath the clear dome that separated them from the atmosphere beyond, they would have seen the usual pools of dull light that had replaced bright stars since The Pollution. Beneath the dome, in the concrete structure that had become their new home, Finn and his father, Patrick Carey, played Robot Wars on the main screen of the family quarters, while Mrs. Caitlin Carey constructed solar garments on the table in the corner.

"I'll beat you yet!" shouted Mr. Carey, clicking frantically on his controller as the boy did the same, eyes glued to the screen. Caitlin sighed and applied new glue to the seams of the garment in front of her.

"You should stop this silliness and get to bed," she warned. "The sun will be coming up in just a few hours. I'll be turning in soon myself."

"I've got you!" shouted Finn, pressing one final button on his controller. The screen exploded in victory lights and then went dark. Finn grinned at his father, ignoring his mother's warning of imminent danger.

"We can't turn in yet," Patrick grumbled, tossing his controller to the floor. "He's still on his way."

Just then a chime sang from the dome, and the old man rose to open the hatch.

"He's here," breathed Finn, scrambling to stand near the entryway. The visitor entered and removed his shiny outer garments just inside the dome. He then stepped into the family quarters and introduced himself as Captain Burns.

"The solar rays are getting hotter," he told them, over a rare and refreshing glass of ice water. "I've been told there's a way to survive outside the domes, but no one has tried it yet."

"Tell us what it is!" Mr. Carey said eagerly, and then began coughing. The visitor waited until he'd stopped.

"The answer lies here," the captain said, pulling a small, silver box from his pocket. "But as I said, no one has tried it yet. Well—without eluding the rays entirely." He coughed as well, and Mrs. Carey let out a barely audible giggle.

"How does it work?" asked Finn, eyes wide as he stared at the glistening box.

"It's designed to act as a personal shield. But, I'm not sure it's feasible. As I believe I've said, I wouldn't recommend trying it, even with the food supplies running so low."

Patrick reached for the box, and Finn's eyes followed as his father held it up in his palm.

"We're very hungry, captain," Mr. Carey said, flipping open the lid of the box to examine the buttons below. "Please, tell us how it works."

As the family gathered around, Captain Burns carefully explained to Mr. Carey how the device worked. Finn could feel both excitement and apprehension as Captain Burns methodically described what each button was for, and the consequences of making the wrong choice.

"I know this is asking a lot," Mr. Carey said nervously, "but let me try this device. I realize it's never worked successfully before, but I'm willing to take the risk. My family will soon need food, and this is our only chance."

Avoiding Mr. Carey's eyes, Captain Burns reluctantly shook his head, yes. Holding the box in his hands, Mr. Carey pulled it tightly to his chest. He prayed that he had made a sensible decision.

STUDYSYNC LIBRARY | Extended Writing Project

 THINK QUESTIONS

1. What is the setting of this narrative? Identify two or more textual details that help identify the setting, and explain why you think the student included them. What does the setting tell you about the kind of story this is?

2. Describe the conflict, or main problem, of this story. Explain which details reveal the conflict, and explain why you think the student has chosen to include these details.

3. What suspenseful elements do you detect in this first reading of the student model narrative? How do these elements add to your interest in the story?

4. As you consider the writing prompt, which selections or other resources would you like to examine to help you create your own narrative?

5. Based on what you have read, listened to, or researched, how would you answer the question, *What attracts us to stories of suspense?*

STUDYSYNC LIBRARY | Extended Writing Project

SKILL: ORGANIZE NARRATIVE WRITING

 ## DEFINE

Every narrative plot contains a **conflict,** or problem the characters must face. The conflict in a narrative is often developed throughout the story and revealed over time. A story's conflict builds to a climax or turning point, when the **characters**—the people or players in the narrative—are forced to take action.

This problem is presented by a **narrator,** who serves as the voice of the story. The narrator can tell the story in the first-person point of view (as a participant in the story) or in the third-person point of view (as an outside observer). The narrator serves as the reader's eyes, allowing readers to view the actions of the story.

Through the narrator, authors introduce characters and reveal details about their relationships to one another as the story unfolds. Characters are the driving force of a story. Their actions, thoughts, and dialogue move the plot forward as they encounter conflict and seek a resolution. Characters develop throughout a story and often undergo a significant change by the story's end.

 ## IDENTIFICATION AND APPLICATION

- A story's narrator helps to orient readers with the details of the story, such as where and when the story takes place and who the story is about.
- Writers reveal information about characters over time, to help readers know and understand the players in the story.
- Writers build stories around a conflict that is interesting to readers. The conflict may be internal (within a character) or external (the character faces an outside force).
- As the story unfolds, writers introduce more details to develop the problem and keep the reader engaged with the characters.
- Narrative writers often introduce elements of suspense to keep a reader guessing about what will happen next. In many suspense stories, writers

Reading & Writing Companion

add a detail that creates an additional problem, or conflict, for a character already facing one problem. This is called heightened conflict, and it works to intensify and increase the tension in the story.

- The sequence of events in a story builds to climax, the point at which the characters are forced to take action or make a decision.

MODEL

Cujo is a fictional narrative, so the author is able to invent the situation in which the characters will face a conflict or problem. In this excerpt from the novel, author Stephen King has placed a mother and son in a closed garage with a rabid dog that is ready to attack. The story begins:

> She reached the front of the hood and started to cross in front of the Pinto, and that was when she heard a new sound. A low, thick growling.
>
> She stopped, her head coming up at once, trying to pinpoint the source of that sound. For a moment she couldn't and she was suddenly terrified, not by the sound itself, but by its seeming directionlessness. It was nowhere. It was everywhere. And then some internal radar—survival equipment, perhaps—turned on all the way, and she understood that the growling was coming from inside the garage.
>
> "Mommy?" Tad poked his head out his open window as far as the seatbelt harness would allow.
>
> "I can't get this damn old—"
>
> "Shhh!"
>
> (growling)

Here, the author has introduced two characters, a woman and her son, Tad. He has also introduced the problem: a growling noise alerts the woman that she and her son are in danger. The reader can also determine that the narrator of this story holds a third-person point of view. The narrator describes the woman's thoughts and actions not as a participant in the story, but as an outside observer. The narrator also reveals details about the scene that heighten the problem: When Tad pokes his head out of the car, the reader learns that the child is inside of the car, while his mother is outside. King writes that the mother "reached the front of the hood, and started to cross in front of the Pinto," which is the name of a car made by the Ford Motor Company in the 1970s. The story then continues:

> She took a tentative step backward, her right hand resting lightly on the Pinto's low hood, her nerves on tripwires as thin as filaments, not

panicked but in a state of heightened alertness, thinking: *It didn't growl before.*

Cujo came out of Joe Camber's garage. Donna stared at him, feeling her breath come to a painless and yet complete stop in her throat. It was the same dog. It was Cujo. But—

But oh my

(oh my God)

The dog's eyes settled on hers. They were red and rheumy. They were leaking some viscous substance. The dog seemed to be weeping gummy tears. His tawny coat was caked and matted with mud and—

Blood. is that

(it is it's blood . . .)

Now the author has given the woman a name, Donna. He has also introduced another character—Cujo, the source of the conflict.

The author includes Donna's thoughts, in italics, to disclose what she is thinking as she stares at Cujo. She is shocked, and her terror grows as she begins to understand the severity of her problem. The thought "It didn't growl before" lets the reader know that Donna has encountered Cujo in the past, and the dog did not present a problem at that time. However, the dog has changed, and Donna and her son are now in danger.

Readers can also infer that Cujo's owner, Joe Camber, is dead, although the narrator does not directly state this as a fact. Cujo "came out of Joe Camber's garage," and Donna soon realizes that Cujo's coat is "caked and matted with mud and—*blood.*" The reader can now assume that the dog is a killer, and he is growling at Donna as she stands outside of her car. As you read on, you will see that certain events cause the conflict between Donna and Cujo to heighten, or intensify, at different points in the story.

 PRACTICE

Name your three favorite suspenseful stories. For each story, identify what conflict or problem the character or characters face and what narrative point of view the story uses to introduce, develop, and heighten this conflict. Describe any trends or patterns you notice in what kinds of conflicts and which type of narrator you find most interesting or engaging as a reader. Doing so may help you identify the kind of suspenseful story you want to tell. Exchange your work with a partner to give and receive feedback about your ideas.

STUDYSYNC LIBRARY | Extended Writing Project

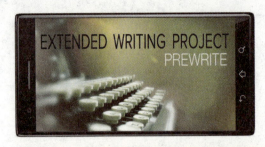

PREWRITE

WRITING PROMPT

You have been reading and learning about stories of suspense, in addition to studying techniques authors use to generate a feeling of suspense in readers. Now you will use those techniques to write your own suspenseful narrative based on real or imagined experiences and events.

Your essay should include:

- a plot with a beginning, middle, and end
- a clear setting
- characters and dialogue
- a suspenseful theme

In addition to studying techniques authors use to entertain readers, you have been reading and learning about stories that contain elements of suspense. In the extended writing project, you will use those narrative writing techniques to compose your own suspenseful narrative.

Writers often take notes about story ideas before they sit down to write. Often, writers like to work in a specific genre, such as science fiction. Some writers list ideas about characters, plot, and setting, and then choose the ones that will be most entertaining for readers. Others start with a conclusion and then map out situations that will lead the characters to the predetermined end of the story.

- Think about what you've learned so far about organizing narrative writing to help you begin prewriting.
  - In what sort of genre would you like to write? Genres include science fiction, horror, romance, fantasy, adventure and detective fiction, to name some examples. Most any genre can include suspense.

- > What types of characters would you like to write about in your suspenseful narrative?
- > What kinds of problems might these characters face? How might the setting of your story affect the characters and problem?
- > What events will lead to the resolution of the conflict while keeping a reader in suspense?
- > From which point of view should your story be told, and why?

- Make a list of answers to these questions by completing the "Prewrite: Narrative Writing" graphic organizer. Record your brainstorming ideas about character, conflict, setting, and narrator on the chart. Then examine your ideas and choose the details that you think will work best for your suspenseful narrative. Here is the chart below, completed by the writer of the student model narrative. Make a fresh chart to help guide your prewriting:

PREWRITE – NARRATIVE WRITING

Characters	Conflict	Setting	Narrator
What types of characters would I like to write about?	What types of problems might these characters face?	How might the setting affect the characters and the problem?	From which point of view should this story be told? Why?
A family—mother, father, ~~daughter,~~ and son ~~Teenage friends~~ ~~An elderly man~~ A mysterious stranger (good for element of suspense—potential for conflict)	Parents struggling to provide for a family ~~Children getting along with one another~~ Outside forces threatening the characters' well-being ("man versus environment"—good for suspense because the outcome is unpredictable; room to create engaging character experiences) ~~Friends who aren't seeing eye to eye~~ ~~A man who discovers something he thought was true is not true after all~~	A futuristic setting could create an interesting "man versus environment" conflict—maybe the family can't go outside because the environment is too unstable (the sun is getting hotter? ~~no more oxygen to breathe?)~~ (good for suspense—readers will wonder what will happen to my characters in this setting; good basis for creating interesting imagined experiences) ~~A modern setting could bring modern issues/a current conflict into play~~	Third-person narrator, so that 1) I can reveal character thoughts if I think it will add to the suspense of the story; and 2) I can more easily discuss the setting details to help describe a science fiction plot.

STUDYSYNC LIBRARY | **Extended Writing Project**

SKILL: INTRODUCTIONS

DEFINE

The **introduction** is the opening of the story, which sets the stage for the events that follow. Because the introduction of a narrative is the reader's first experience with a particular story, writers often include elements of **exposition**—essential information such as character, setting, and problem—in the opening paragraphs of the story. A story's introduction should capture a reader's attention and tempt the reader to move forward into the story with interest. After reading a story's introduction, a reader should think, "I wonder what will happen in this story. I'd like to keep reading and discover more about these characters." A good introduction hooks a reader with precise language and sensory details that transport a reader into the world of the story.

IDENTIFICATION AND APPLICATION

- The beginning, or introduction of a narrative includes **exposition.** The exposition introduces and establishes the setting, the narrator, and the characters. It frequently provides clues about the genre. For example, a science fiction story could include details that let readers know that the narrative is set in the future.

- As in other forms of writing, authors of narrative fiction often use a "hook" to grab a reader's interest. In a narrative, a hook can be an exciting moment, a detailed description, or a surprising or thoughtful comment made by the narrator or the main character.

- The beginning of a narrative also establishes the story structure an author intends to use. For example, some suspense stories begin with a flashback. This strategy "grabs" the reader's attention and builds suspense by making the reader wonder what's going on. Most stories, however, start at the beginning, introduce a conflict, and relate the events in time order. They use descriptive supporting details, engaging characters, and unexpected plot twists to keep readers interested.

MODEL

In the opening paragraphs of a narrative, a writer aims to engage and orient, or familiarize, readers with specific details. These details often reveal important information about the characters and setting of the story, and a hint of what the conflict or problem might be. The author of "The Monkey's Paw," W.W. Jacobs, introduces the story as follows:

> Without, **the night was cold and wet,** but in the **small parlour of Laburnam Villa** the **blinds were drawn** and the **fire burned brightly. Father and son** were at chess, the former, who **possessed ideas about the game involving radical changes, putting his king into such sharp and unnecessary perils** that it even **provoked comment** from **the white-haired old lady** knitting placidly by the fire.

Here the author introduces the setting—a "small parlour of Laburnam Villa"—and gives the reader sensory details to help place the reader in the opening scene. The reader knows that it is a "cold and wet" night outside, but in contrast, the family has created a cozy atmosphere inside with "drawn" blinds and a "bright" fire. These sensory details help the reader see the scene in his or her mind and draw the reader into the story.

The author also introduces the characters—"father and son," and "the white-haired old lady"—though he does not name them. Jacobs also gives the reader clues about the personalities of these characters. The father "possessed ideas about the game [of chess] involving radical changes" and put "his king into such sharp and unnecessary perils" that it prompts the old woman to comment. These details reveal to readers that the father is a bit reckless and headstrong, while the old woman is more cautious. These hints are meant to tempt the reader to wonder, "Who are these characters?" and "How will these character traits play into the plot of the story?" A reader might also think, "This setting is peaceful. When will the conflict arise?" The author hopes the reader will want to read on to find out the answers to these questions.

PRACTICE

Write an introduction for your suspenseful narrative that reveals information about the story's setting and characters. When you are finished, trade with a partner and offer each other feedback. How precise is the language used in your partner's introduction? Do the details help you to picture the setting and characters? What information about the characters is revealed in the introduction? Were you interested in what would happen next? Offer each other suggestions, and remember that they are most helpful when they are constructive.

STUDYSYNC LIBRARY | Extended Writing Project

SKILL: NARRATIVE TECHNIQUES AND SEQUENCING

 DEFINE

When writing a story, authors use a variety of narrative techniques to develop both the plot and the characters, explore the setting, and engage the reader. These techniques include dialogue, a sequencing of events, pacing, and description. **Dialogue,** what the characters say to one another, is often used to develop characters and move the events of the plot forward. Every narrative contains a **sequence of events,** which is carefully planned and controlled by the author as the story unfolds. Writers often manipulate the **pacing** of a narrative, or the speed with which events occur, to slow down or speed up the action at certain points in a story. This can create tension and suspense. Writers use **description** to build story details and reveal information about the characters, setting, and plot.

The beginning of a story is called the **introduction** or **exposition.** This is the part of the story in which the writer provides the reader with essential information, introducing the characters, the time and place in which the action occurs, and the problem or conflict the characters must face and attempt to solve.

As the story continues, the writer includes details and events to develop the conflict and move the story forward. These events—known as the **rising action** of the story—build until the story reaches its **climax.** This is a turning point in the story, where the most exciting and intense action usually occurs. It is also the point at which the characters begin to find a solution to the problem or conflict in the plot.

The writer then focuses on details and events that make up the **falling action** of the story. This is everything that happens after the climax, leading to a **resolution.** These elements make up a story's **conclusion,** which often contains a message or final thought for the reader.

STUDYSYNC LIBRARY | **Extended Writing Project**

IDENTIFICATION AND APPLICATION

- A narrative outline can help writers organize a sequence of events before they begin writing a story.
- A narrative outline should follow this framework:
  > exposition, rising action (conflict), climax, falling action, resolution

- The exposition contains essential information for the reader, such as characters, setting, and the problem or conflict the characters will face.
  > Settings are shown in descriptions and can influence events.
  > Writers often include details to reveal the elements of the exposition without directly stating these elements for the reader.
  > Readers should feel interested during the exposition and wonder "What will happen in this story?"

- In the rising action, a writer begins to develop plot and character.
  > Characters are developed through dialogue, action, and description.
  > The rising action introduces and builds on the conflict until the story reaches the climax.
  > During the rising action, readers should feel invested in the story and care about what is going to happen next.

- The climax is the turning point in the story, often where the most exciting action takes place.
  > Pacing is a technique writers use to control the speed of the way events are revealed.
  > The events that take place during the climax often force characters into action.
  > Readers should feel tense or excited during the climax and wonder, "How will the characters move forward?"

- The details and events that follow the climax make up the falling action of the story.
  > The events that take place during the climax should lead to the resolution.
  > During the falling action, readers should feel anxious to know how the story will end and wonder, "How will the conflict be resolved?"

- The story must end in resolution of the conflict.
  > The way the problem and developed and moves toward resolution should be logical and feel natural to the story.
  > The resolution should explain—with no room for doubt—how the characters resolved the conflict.

> By the end of the story, readers should feel satisfied and entertained and think, "That was a great story!"

MODEL

In the story "The Monkey's Paw," author W.W. Jacobs uses narrative techniques and sequencing to develop both the characters in the story and the events of the plot. Look at this excerpt, which occurs just after Sergeant-Major Morris has left the White family home:

> "Did you give him anything for it, father?" inquired Mrs. White, **regarding her husband closely.**
>
> "A trifle," said he, **colouring slightly.** "He didn't want it, but I made him take it. And he pressed me again to throw it away."
>
> "Likely," said Herbert, **with pretended horror.** "Why, we're going to be rich, and famous, and happy. Wish to be an emperor, father, to begin with; then you can't be henpecked."
>
> He darted round the table, pursued by the maligned Mrs. White armed with an antimacassar.
>
> Mr. White took the paw from his pocket and eyed it **dubiously.** "I don't know what to wish for, and that's a fact," he said slowly. **"It seems to me I've got all I want."**

In this exchange of dialogue, the author provides many key details that reveal character traits. When Mrs. White asks her husband if he has paid for the monkey's paw, she is "regarding him closely." This signals her worry that her husband has foolishly spent the family's money, and that perhaps he has done so before. It also lets readers know that the family is not wealthy, and that money is a concern in the White household. Mr. White tells his wife that he has paid a small amount, "colouring slightly." Mr. White's flushed face indicates that his wife's concern is justified, and that he has probably paid too much for the paw after all.

Herbert's "pretended horror" as he mocks the power of the monkey's paw shows that he is good-humored—and perhaps foolish. As Herbert teases his parents, the scene becomes light and playful. Then Mr. White takes the paw from his pocket and eyes it "dubiously," revealing his uncertainty about its powers. "I don't know what to wish for, and that's a fact," Mr. White says, and the author notes that he says this slowly, as he considers whether he should bother wishing at all. White's statement "It seems to me I've got all I want" not

STUDYSYNC LIBRARY | Extended Writing Project

only reveals the fact that, basically, he is satisfied with his life, but it also sets up the events to come in the story. Will he or won't he make a wish? The author draws out the suspense.

As the rising action of the story continues, Mr. White makes his first wish:

"I wish for two hundred pounds," said the old man distinctly.

A fine crash from the piano greeted the words, interrupted by **a shuddering cry** from the old man. **His wife and son ran toward him.**

"It moved," he cried, with a glance of **disgust** at the object as it lay on the floor. "As I wished **it twisted in my hands like a snake.**"

Here the pacing of the story quickens as the author changes the tone of the scene and presents readers with sensory details and character action. "A fine crash from the piano" and the old man's "shuddering cry" are jarring to both characters and readers, who are eager to see what will happen after Mr. White makes his wish. Herbert and his mother spring into action and rush toward Mr. White, who—once "dubious"—now looks at the paw with "disgust." His revelation that the paw "twisted" in his hands "like a snake" suggests to the characters—and to readers—that the paw might have powers after all. The author then slows the pacing of the story again as the scene continues:

"Well, I don't see the money," said his son, as he picked it up and placed it on the table, "and I bet I never shall."

"It must have been your fancy, father," said his wife, regarding him **anxiously.**

He shook his head. "Never mind, though; there's no harm done, but it gave me a shock all the same."

They sat down by the fire again while the two men finished their pipes. Outside, **the wind was higher than ever,** and the old man **started nervously at the sound of a door banging upstairs. A silence unusual and depressing** settled upon all three, which lasted until the old couple rose to retire for the night.

Though the pacing of the action has slowed, the author includes details that reveal the characters' oppression as they attempt to convince themselves that the paw holds no formidable power. The characters act "anxiously" and "nervously" as they settle into an "unusual and depressing" silence. The wind, "higher than ever," and the sound of a banging door upstairs are sensory details, often associated with spooky houses, which set both readers and the characters in the story on edge as the scene comes to a close. By using these narrative techniques, the author has crafted a suspenseful scene that points the story toward its climax. A outline of the story's rising action might look as follows:

I. Rising Action
   A. Mrs. White asks what her husband spent on paw, suggesting her fear that he has spent too much.
   B. Mr. White blushes, which suggests that he did and feels somewhat sheepish about it.
   C. Herbert teases his parents to show that that he does not take the paw seriously.
   D. Mr. White muses aloud that he is basically content and does not have anything to wish for.
   E. At last, Mr. White wishes for 200 pounds.
   F. Mr. White cries out that the paw moved, which startles and alarms his family.
   G. The pleasant mood of the evening is destroyed; Mr. and Mrs. White feel anxious.

PRACTICE

Create an outline of the sequence of events that might make up the rising action in your suspenseful narrative. As you create your outline, consider the characters, conflict, setting, and narrative point of view you identified in the Prewrite stage and the exposition you began to develop in your introduction. What events will follow this introduction and form your story's rising action? How might you use pacing to propel the action and advance the plot in this part of the narrative? When you are finished, exchange outlines with a partner to offer and receive feedback.

STUDYSYNC LIBRARY | Extended Writing Project

PLAN

WRITING PROMPT

You have been reading and learning about stories of suspense, in addition to studying techniques authors use to generate a feeling of suspense in readers. Now you will use those techniques to write your own suspenseful narrative based on real or imagined experiences and events.

Your essay should include:

- a plot with a beginning, middle, and end
- a clear setting
- characters and dialogue
- a suspenseful theme

In preparing to write your suspenseful narrative, you have learned about organizing narrative writing. This helped you brainstorm ideas to complete your prewriting. Now you will consider the elements of a narrative outline that you explored in the Narrative Techniques and Sequencing lesson to help plan your writing.

To begin planning the main action of your own suspenseful narrative, review your prewriting and ask yourself the following questions:

- What details and events are most important in the exposition of a story?
- What story developments should take place during the rising action of a story?
- What is the purpose of a story's climax? What might my own story's climax be?
- What can I do to lead readers toward the resolution of a story? How do I want my story to resolve?

- What narrative techniques would be most effective in creating a feeling of suspense?

Use the StudySync "Narrative Writing Plot Diagram" to plan a complete sequence of events for your suspenseful narrative. You may include or revise the rising action events you brainstormed earlier. The plot diagram below was completed by the writer of the student model narrative. Use a blank version of the model to help guide your planning:

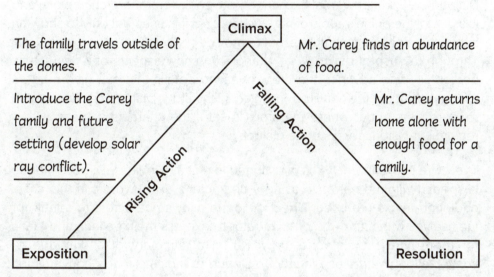

SKILL: WRITING DIALOGUE

DEFINE

Dialogue is a written verbal exchange between two or more characters, and it is one of the primary tools of narrative writing. It is used not only to show an interaction between characters, but to provide readers with important details. Through the use of dialogue, an author can show aspects of a character's personality and advance the plot, revealing details that can give readers information about the conflict or problem in the story. Dialogue can even give readers hints about where the story is set if the characters speak with a regional or historically accurate dialect.

There are two different types of dialogue: direct and indirect. Direct dialogue is speech within a narrative using a character's *exact* words. In this case, quotation marks are used. Direct dialogue allows characters to speak for themselves without relying on a narrator to express their feelings and ideas for them. Indirect dialogue, however, is a summary of a dialogue or conversation. Writers use indirect dialogue to indicate that a conversation took place, but the exact words that were spoken are unimportant. Readers only need to know that the conversation occurred and, generally, what it was about.

No matter what type of dialogue a writer uses, however, it is important that punctuation is used appropriately so that the reader understands who is speaking.

IDENTIFICATION AND APPLICATION

Here are a few basic guidelines to follow when using dialogue in your narrative:

- Use open (") and closed (") quotation marks to indicate the words that are spoken by the characters.
- Always begin a new paragraph when the speaker changes.

- Make sure the reader knows who is saying what.
- When crafting an interaction between characters, the author can use more phrases than simply "he said" or "she said." Depending on the nature or emotion of a character's dialogue, it can be followed by stronger verbs, adjectives, or adverbs, such as "whispered" or "exclaimed loudly."
- Use correct punctuation marks and capitalization. Periods and commas always go inside quotation marks.

Writers can use both direct and indirect dialogue to develop characters by showcasing the characters' opinions, reactions, emotions, experiences, personalities, and even appearances through:

- What the characters say (direct or indirect speech)
- How the characters say it (their speech patterns; the expressions and language they use)
- The way the characters say it (angrily, happily, etc.)
- The characters' body language, actions, and thoughts as they are speaking

MODEL

Read the following excerpt from "The Monkey's Paw," by W.W. Jacobs to see how the author effectively uses direct dialogue:

> **"Hark at the wind,"** said Mr. White, who, having seen a fatal mistake after it was too late, was amiably desirous of preventing his son from seeing it.
>
> **"I'm listening,"** said the latter, grimly surveying the board as he stretched out his hand. **"Check."**
>
> "I should hardly think that he'd come to-night," said his father, with his hand poised over the board.
>
> "Mate," replied the son.
>
> **"That's the worst of living so far out,"** bawled Mr. White, with sudden and unlooked-for violence; **"of all the beastly, slushy, out-of-the-way places to live in, this is the worst. Pathway's a bog, and the road's a torrent.** I don't know what people are thinking about. I suppose because only two houses in the road are let, they think it doesn't matter."
>
> **"Never mind, dear,"** said his wife, soothingly; **"perhaps you'll win the next one."**

In this excerpt the author has followed all of the technical guidelines regarding direct dialogue. He sets off the direct speech of each character with open quotation marks and places the closed quotation mark outside the end punctuation of the quote, while the rest of the sentence has its own end punctuation. He also begins a new paragraph when the speaker changes.

But notice what else the author does with dialogue. When his son wins the chess game, Mr. White suddenly explodes "with sudden and unlooked for violence," complaining about living "so far out" in a "beastly, slushy, out-of-the-way place." His wife, however, knows that though her husband is complaining about the location of their house and the weather, he "explodes" because he is really angry about losing the game. So she responds, "Never mind, dear, perhaps you'll win the next one." It is through dialogue, then, that the author reveals one of Mr. White's character traits. He is very competitive, and he does not like to lose at chess.

Now let's look at another excerpt to see how the author uses indirect dialogue:

> The sergeant-major shook hands, and taking the proffered seat by the fire, watched contentedly while his host got out whiskey and tumblers and stood a small copper kettle on the fire.
>
> **At the third glass his eyes got brighter, and he began to talk,** the little family circle regarding with eager interest this visitor from distant parts, as he squared his broad shoulders in the chair **and spoke of wild scenes and doughty deeds; of wars and plagues and strange peoples.**

Within this excerpt, the author uses indirect dialogue to introduce readers to the character Sergeant-Major Morris. We can see that he is lively and enjoys being social and telling stories. Though he has known Mr. White for many years, he now seems exotic to the White family as "a visitor from distant parts." It is Sergeant-Major Morris who will pass the monkey's paw onto the White family, but first he speaks of "wild scenes" and the "strange peoples" he has met in his travels. Readers need to know that this conversation took place to set the scene for what is to follow, but it is not important to know the exact words that were spoken.

Finally, let's explore the third excerpt to see how the author uses dialogue, as well as verbs, adverbs, and adjectives, to help develop character.

> "Nothing," said the soldier, hastily. "Leastways nothing worth hearing."
>
> "Monkey's paw?" **said Mrs. White, curiously.**

"Well, it's **just a bit of what you might call magic, perhaps**," said the sergeant-major, offhandedly.

His three listeners **leaned forward eagerly.** The visitor absent-mindedly put his empty glass to his lips and then set it down again. His host filled it for him.

"To look at," **said the sergeant-major, fumbling in his pocket** "it's just an ordinary little paw, dried to a mummy."

Readers can tell that Sergeant-Major Morris does not wish to talk about the monkey's paw—they can tell because the author uses the words "hastily" and "offhandedly" to describe Morris's manner of speaking. He knows how powerful and dangerous the monkey's paw can be and he is trying to protect the White family from the temptation. The Whites, however, are fascinated. Mrs. White asks her question in a curious tone of voice, and the entire family "leans forward eagerly" to listen to the sergeant-major's tale. Though it is clear that Morris is uncomfortable talking about it, Mr. White fills his glass as soon as he sets it down. This indicates that he is encouraging Morris to stay and continue talking. The sergeant-major fumbles for the monkey's paw in his pocket as he speaks, indicating a nervousness to continue.

Through the use of dialogue in these excerpts from "The Monkey's Paw" readers learn not only what the characters discussed, but also what they are like and how they feel at different points in the story.

 PRACTICE

Write a scene for your suspenseful narrative in which two or more characters engage in both direct and indirect dialogue. When you are finished, trade with a partner and offer each other feedback. Has the writer followed the technical guidelines relating to direct dialogue? Are there areas where the indirect dialogue can be improved? How does the dialogue help develop the characters? Does the dialogue reveal information about the plot? Offer each other suggestions, and remember that they are most helpful when they are constructive.

STUDYSYNC LIBRARY | **Extended Writing Project**

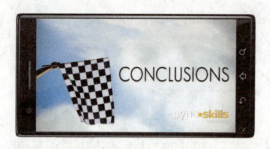

SKILL: CONCLUSIONS

DEFINE

At the climax of a story, the main character or characters figure out a way to solve the problem or conflict in the plot. But the story isn't over yet. The falling action in a work of literature is the sequence of events that follow the climax and end in the conclusion of the story. The **conclusion** ends all action within the plot, and provides a resolution of the conflict or problem in the story. A story's conclusion often communicates a lesson that the characters have learned—one that will benefit a reader to learn as well. This is the theme of the story. Because the conclusion is the author's farewell to the reader, an author must consider how the conclusion will affect the reader, as well as how to leave him or her with a lasting impression of the story.

IDENTIFICATION AND APPLICATION

- A narrative conclusion includes the last events in the story, including:
  › A final interaction between characters who have faced the main problem or conflict in the story.
  › The final thoughts of the character(s) and/or narrator.

- An effective narrative conclusion presents a resolution of the conflict in the story. It should tell clearly how the characters resolved the conflict or problem or how it was resolved for them.

- The way a problem is resolved can be a surprise to the reader, particularly in a suspense story, but it should still be logical and feel like a natural part of the plot.

- At the end of the story, the reader should be able to think about the narrator's role—how his or her point of view affected the way the story was told.

- A strong narrative conclusion leaves the reader with a lasting impression, and often wraps up the theme of the story.

MODEL

In Edgar Allan Poe's story "The Tell-Tale Heart" the narrator describes his sensitivity to the old man with whom he lives, and particularly to his "evil eye," which has kept the narrator awake night after night. The story builds to a moment of climax when the narrator murders the old man and buries his body beneath the floorboards of the house.

Though the narrator now believes he has resolved his problem, the falling action of the story takes place afterward. As the narrator entertains the police officers who have come to investigate the old man's shriek, Poe presents the falling action that will lead to the actual resolution of the conflict:

> No doubt I now grew **VERY pale;** but I talked more fluently, and with a **heightened voice.** Yet the sound increased — and what could I do? It was **A LOW, DULL, QUICK SOUND — MUCH SUCH A SOUND AS A WATCH MAKES WHEN ENVELOPED IN COTTON.** I gasped for breath, and yet the officers heard it not. I talked more quickly, more vehemently but the noise steadily increased. I arose and argued about trifles, in a **high key** and with **violent gesticulations;** but the noise steadily increased. Why WOULD they not be gone? I paced the floor to and fro with **heavy strides,** as if excited to fury by the observations of the men, but the noise steadily increased. O God! what COULD I do? I foamed — I raved — I swore! **I swung the chair upon which I had been sitting, and grated it upon the boards,** but the noise arose over all and continually increased. It grew **louder — louder — louder!** And still the men chatted pleasantly, and smiled. Was it possible they heard not? Almighty God! — no, no? They heard! — they suspected! — they KNEW! — they were making a mockery of my **horror!** — this I thought, and this I think. But anything was better than this **agony!** Anything was more tolerable than this **derision!** I could bear those hypocritical smiles no longer! I felt that I must scream or die! — and now — again — hark! **louder! louder! louder! LOUDER! —**

In this part of the story, Poe shows readers that the narrator's mental unrest is now greater than ever, despite his claims of sanity. Poe uses descriptive details such as the narrator's "very pale" face and "heightened voice" in a "high key" to help readers understand how the narrator is feeling. He uses strong verbs and adjectives such as "violent gesticulations" and "heavy strides" to convey the narrator's increasingly wild actions, until he has reached the point where he has "swung" the chair he was sitting in and "grated" the floorboards to drown out the noise of the beating heart.

Poe also creates a sensory experience for readers in his description of the heartbeat, which begins as "a low, dull, quick sound—much as a sound a watch makes when enveloped in cotton" and grows increasingly "louder! louder! louder!" within the narrator's mind. As the heartbeat grows and the narrator comes undone in front of the police, readers may find their own heartbeats quickened with anxiety over the narrator's situation. Poe then brings the action and narrative to a halt, frightening in its suddenness, with a final statement made by the narrator:

> **"Villains!" I shrieked,** "dissemble no more! I admit the deed! — **tear up the planks!** — here, here! — it is **the beating of his hideous heart!"**

Though the officers have been calmly chatting with the narrator, unaware of his guilt, the narrator has convinced himself that they are scheming "villains" who are waiting for a confession. When the unexpected confession comes—with the narrator's emotional request to "tear up the planks" and rid him of the burden he carries—the narrative comes to a halt. The conflict has been resolved; the narrator has confessed to the crime and will no longer be tortured by the beating heart. *Or will he?* a reader might ask after reading the story. Will the narrator's conscience continue to haunt him?

"The Tell-Tale Heart" contains one of the most memorable conclusions of all-time. The author's pacing—crafted carefully through repetition and the narrator's frantic thoughts—and rich descriptions of the narrator's building mental distress allow readers to journey into madness. Anxious, excited, shaken, upset—no matter how an individual reader feels after reading the story's conclusion, Poe took care to ensure that his story left readers with a lasting impression of their reading experience. One theme in the story is that the human heart cannot endure the burden of guilt, especially in the case of murder. The guilty must confess somehow or be consumed by his or her conscience. The narrator might not learn anything in the story, but the reader does.

DRAFT

WRITING PROMPT

You have been reading and learning about stories of suspense, in addition to studying techniques authors use to generate a feeling of suspense in readers. Now you will use those techniques to write your own suspenseful narrative based on real or imagined experiences and events.

Your essay should include:

- a plot with a beginning, middle, and end
- a clear setting
- characters and dialogue
- a suspenseful theme

You have already made much progress toward writing your suspenseful narrative. You have planned your writing by identifying your characters, conflict, setting, and point of view and developing a sequence of events. You have considered about how writers use descriptive details to enhance and support a narrative. You have drafted your introductory paragraphs and paragraphs containing dialogue, and you have practiced writing the elements of a strong and effective conclusion. You have also considered the elements of suspense writing in relation to audience and purpose. Now it is time to write a draft of your suspenseful narrative.

Use your prewriting graphic organizer, plot diagram, and other prewriting materials to help you as you write. Remember that in the rising action of a narrative, writers introduce characters, setting, and conflict and begin to develop characters and plot. The rising action leads to the story's climax, the turning point in the story, where the most exciting action takes place. The falling action of a story occurs after the climax and leads to the resolution of the conflict and the story's conclusion. Keep readers in mind as you write, and aim to keep your audience engaged and in suspense.

When drafting, ask yourself these questions:

- What can I do to improve my introduction so that readers understand expository information—including character, conflict, setting, and point of view—early on in my story?
- How logical is the sequence of events I have established in my story?
- How can I use dialogue and description to reveal information about characters and advance the plot?
- How can I use pacing to build suspense in my story?
- What details can I improve and expand on to create a vivid experience for readers?
- How will I resolve the story's conflict in a way that is satisfying and memorable to readers?

Before you submit your draft, read it over carefully. You want to be sure that you've responded to all aspects of the prompt.

STUDYSYNC LIBRARY | Extended Writing Project

SKILL: TRANSITIONS

DEFINE

Transitions are words or phrases that help carry a thought from one sentence to another, from one idea to another, or from one paragraph to another. Good transitions can act as bridges, and turn disconnected, "choppy" writing into a unified whole that flows smoothly from one point or event to another. Transitions between events in a plot can help readers understand how certain events are related and work together in a story, building toward a climax. In narrative stories, transitional devices usually take the form of time order words and phrases that show the relationships between events. They can also signal a change in the setting, or where a story takes place.

IDENTIFICATION AND APPLICATION

- Transitional devices link sentences and paragraphs together smoothly so that there are no sudden jumps or breaks between events or ideas. Writers can also use transitions to show the relationships between character experiences and story events.
- There are several types of transitional devices, and each category leads readers to make certain connections.
- Transitional words and phrases to indicate time has passed include *immediately, thereafter, soon, after a few hours* (or days, weeks, etc.), *finally, then, later, previously, formerly, first* (second, etc.), *next,* and *then.*
- To indicate a sequence of events, writers often use transitional words and phrases such as *next, following this, at this time, now, at this point, after, afterward, subsequently, finally, consequently, previously,* and *just then.*
- To show differences or exceptions between characters and events in a narrative, authors sometimes use transitional words and phrases such as *yet, still, however, nevertheless, in spite of, despite, of course, once in a while,* or *sometimes.*

STUDYSYNC LIBRARY | **Extended Writing Project**

MODEL

This excerpt from "The Monkey's Paw," contains transitions that help the reader understand the setting and sequence of events. Read the passages to identify the transitions the author used.

> **In the huge new cemetery,** some two miles distant, the old people buried their dead, and came back to a house steeped in shadow and silence. It was all over so quickly that at first they could hardly realize it, and remained in a state of expectation as though of something else to happen —something else which was to lighten this load, too heavy for old hearts to bear.
>
> **But the days passed,** and expectation gave place to resignation—the hopeless resignation of the old, sometimes miscalled, apathy. Sometimes they hardly exchanged a word, for now they had nothing to talk about, and their days were long to weariness.
>
> **It was about a week after that the old man, waking suddenly in the night, stretched out his hand and found himself alone.** The room was in darkness, and the sound of subdued weeping came from the window. He raised himself in bed and listened.

In the first paragraph from this excerpt, the author uses the transition "In the huge cemetery," to indicate that the action in the story has moved from its previous location (the home of the old couple) to the cemetery where they have just buried their son. In the next paragraph, the transition "But the days passed" helps the reader understand that some time has gone by since the burial, and the old man and woman have become hopeless, and hardly speak to one another. The author then moves the action to the present with the sentence "It was about a week after that the old man, waking suddenly in the night, stretched out his hand and found himself alone." The rest of the action, and the conclusion of the story, will take place that night, after the man wakes up.

PRACTICE

Write one body paragraph for your suspenseful narrative that uses transition words and/or phrases. When you are finished, trade with a partner and offer each other feedback. How effective are the transitions at indicating the passage of time? How well do the transitions show relationships among character experiences and story events? Offer each other constructive, helpful suggestions for revision.

REVISE

WRITING PROMPT

You have been reading and learning about stories of suspense, in addition to studying techniques authors use to generate a feeling of suspense in readers. Now you will use those techniques to write your own suspenseful narrative based on real or imagined experiences and events.

Your essay should include:

- a plot with a beginning, middle, and end
- a clear setting
- characters and dialogue
- a suspenseful theme

You have written a draft of your suspenseful narrative. You have also received input from your peers about how to improve it. Now you are going to revise your draft.

Here are some recommendations to help you revise:

- Review the suggestions made by your peers. Decide which ones you want to include.
- Examine the introduction to your narrative.
  › Do your introductory paragraphs contain helpful expository information about your characters?
  › Does the introduction establish a narrative point of view?
  › Does your story's introduction orient the reader in the time and place of your story's setting?
  › Have you introduced the conflict in the introductory paragraphs of your narrative?
  › Does your introduction contain details that provide needed information?

- Evaluate the sequencing of events in your narrative.
  - Do the events in your narrative follow a logical order?
  - Have you used transition words and phrases to signal shifts in time or setting and show the relationships among experiences and events?
  - Are your story events organized in a way that creates a sense of suspense for readers?
  - Does the order of events in your narrative help build and develop the conflict in your story?
  - Is the pacing appropriate? Should the pace be quickened or slowed at points to create a sense of urgency or suspense?

- Examine the prose you have used to tell your story.
  - Have you included descriptive, sensory, and precise details that help readers visualize the characters, setting, and events in your narrative?
  - Are there places where you need to add information or details, or where you can eliminate irrelevant details?
  - Do your transitions show the relationships among character experiences and story events?
  - Have you used language that is engaging and exciting for readers?

- Look at the dialogue in your story.
  - Do your characters address one another in direct dialogue?
  - What do details in the dialogue reveal about the characters?
  - Does the dialogue help build the conflict and advance the plot?
  - Does the dialogue reveal additional information about the setting of your narrative?
  - Have you followed the technical guidelines for writing direct and indirect dialogue?
  - Is it clear to readers who is speaking when characters converse in your story?

- Evaluate the conclusion of your story.
  - Does the conclusion present a logical resolution of the conflict?
  - Do you think readers will feel satisfied and entertained after reading your story's conclusion?
  - Have you crafted a conclusion that will leave the reader with a lasting impression of your story?
  - Does your conclusion contain any elements that might elicit an emotional response from a reader?

Use these questions to help you evaluate your suspenseful narrative to determine areas that should be strengthened or improved. Then revise these elements of your narrative.

STUDYSYNC LIBRARY | Extended Writing Project

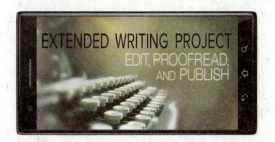

EDIT, PROOFREAD, AND PUBLISH

WRITING PROMPT

You have been reading and learning about stories of suspense, in addition to studying techniques authors use to generate a feeling of suspense in readers. Now you will use those techniques to write your own suspenseful narrative based on real or imagined experiences and events.

Your essay should include:

- a plot with a beginning, middle, and end
- a clear setting
- characters and dialogue
- a suspenseful theme

The final steps to complete your suspenseful narrative are to polish your piece by editing, proofreading, and publishing it. You should have the revised draft that you completed in a previous lesson. Think about all of the lessons in this sequence. As you reread your narrative, be sure to apply what you have learned about audience and purpose, organization of events, descriptive details, writing dialogue, introductions (with exposition), conclusions (with a resolution), and transitions. Review the suggestions that you received from the peer reviews during each step in the process and make sure you have applied them.

Here are some suggestions to guide you through the process of finalizing your essay:

- Now that you are satisfied with your work, proofread for grammar, punctuation, and spelling. Pay special attention to the parts of the essay that you just revised because it is easy to introduce new errors or to accidentally create unclear sentences when you are proofreading and making last-minute corrections.

> › Check each sentence to make sure it is clearly written and punctuated. Check that your dialogue is formatted and punctuated correctly.
> › Be sure you have included appropriate transitions between events or when introducing characters. Check that the transitions are punctuated correctly.
> › Examine your use of verbs. Check to see that your verbs correctly express the intended mood and accurately show the actions or thoughts of the characters.
> › Check the spelling of your work. Look at words that have suffixes to be sure you followed the rules for adding endings properly and that they represent the intended meaning. Check, too, for words whose meanings and spellings are often confused.

- Once your narrative has been proofread and edited, it is time to publish your work. You can add it to your classroom's website or blog, post it on a bulletin board, or share it with family and friends. Be sure to include a list of the works you used for sources, and if you publish online, add links to those resources so that interested readers can gather more information.

PHOTO/IMAGE CREDITS:

Cover, ©iStock.com/MoreISO, ©iStock.com/GiuseppeParisi, ©iStock.com/alexey_boldin, ©iStock.com/skegbydave
p. iii, ©iStock.com/DNY59, ©iStock.com/alexey_boldin, ©iStock.com/LaraBelova
p. iv, E+/Getty Images
p. v, ©iStock.com/moevin, ©iStock.com/skegbydave, ©iStock.com/Chemlamp
p. 2, ©iStock.com/MoreISO
p. 4, ©iStock.com/Kutsuks
p. 9, ©iStock.com/stacey_newman
p. 23, ©iStock.com/Sohl
p. 28, ©iStock.com/urbancow
p. 34, public domain
p. 40, ©iStock.com/THEPALMER
p. 46, ©iStock.com/hidesy
p. 53, Moment Open/Getty Images
p. 60, ©iStock.com/anskuw
p. 68, ©iStock.com/diane555
p. 72, ©iStock.com/southerlycourse
p. 78, ©iStock.com/moevin, ©iStock.com/svariophoto
p. 79, ©iStock.com/moevin, ©iStock.com/skegbydave
p. 83, ©iStock.com/lcsdesign, ©iStock.com/skegbydave
p. 86, ©iStock.com/moevin, ©iStock.com/skegbydave
p. 89, ©iStock.com/bo1982, ©iStock.com/skegbydave
p. 91, ©iStock.com/fotokostic, ©iStock.com/skegbydave
p. 96, ©iStock.com/moevin, ©iStock.com/skegbydave
p. 98, ©iStock.com/chrisphoto1, ©iStock.com/skegbydave
p. 102, ©iStock.com/stevedangers, ©iStock.com/skegbydave
p. 105, ©iStock.com/moevin, ©iStock.com/skegbydave
p. 107, ©iStock.com/Jeff_Hu, ©iStock.com/skegbydave
p. 109, ©iStock.com/moevin, ©iStock.com/skegbydave
p. 111, ©iStock.com/moevin, ©iStock.com/skegbydave

Text Fulfillment Through StudySync

If you are interested in specific titles, please fill out the form below and we will check availability through our partners.

ORDER DETAILS

Date:

TITLE	AUTHOR	Paperback/Hardcover	Specific Edition *If Applicable*	Quantity

SHIPPING INFORMATION

Contact:
Title:
School/District:
Address Line 1:
Address Line 2:
Zip or Postal Code:
Phone:
Mobile:
Email:

BILLING INFORMATION ☐ SAME AS SHIPPING

Contact:
Title:
School/District:
Address Line 1:
Address Line 2:
Zip or Postal Code:
Phone:
Mobile:
Email:

PAYMENT INFORMATION

☐ CREDIT CARD

Name on Card:
Card Number: Expiration Date: Security Code:

☐ PO

Purchase Order Number:

StudySync Text Fulfillment, BookheadEd Learning, LLC
610 Daniel Young Drive | Sonoma, CA 95476